JOSHUA L. CHAMBERLAIN

By Thomas A. Desjardin
Published by Greystone Communications, 1999

GREYSTONE'S
AMERICAN HISTORY
PRODUCTS

TABLE OF CONTENTS

growing up along

Abundant forests and vast, fertile lands attracted many to the shores of the Penobscot River during

SIXTY YEARS AFTER THE AMERICAN REVOLUTION, Bangor, Maine became known as the "the lumber capitol of the world." The town was bustling and dynamic. People from all over the world migrated there seeking prosperity. Lumbermen harvested tall, straight pine trees from the state's bountiful forests and brought them to the banks of

THE PENOBSCOT RIVER

the lumber boom of the 19th century.

he Penobscot River for worldwide shipment. Poor Irish laborers, driven from their

homeland by famine and poverty, survived by accepting grueling jobs. Ship owners and sea

captains made fortunes after a few voyages. All one needed to succeed was an imagination

and a willingness to work.

THE Chamberlains farmed in this community for a few generations. Their 100-acre farm in Brewer, across the river from Bangor, thrived and provided a comfortable living. One of the sons, Joshua L. Chamberlain, Jr., brought his new wife Sarah here. They soon started a family.

Their first child, Lawrence Joshua Chamberlain, arrived on September 8, 1828. A variety of people inspired Joshua and Sarah when they chose their son's name. The middle was for his father and grandfather, while his first name was for Commodore James Lawrence. This sea captain gained fame by declaring, "don't give up the ship" during the heat of an 1813 naval battle. His father picked an appropriate hero. As he grew to manhood, Lawrence faced many challenges with that same type of courage and fortitude.

Soon, four more children joined Lawrence. Horace,

Joshua L. Chamberlain, Jr.

Sarah Chamberlain

Sarah "Sae" Chamberlain

nicknamed "Hod," was born in 1834. A sister, Sarah, or Sae, came in 1836. Two other brothers arrived later: John in 1838 and Tom in 1841. Their lives were much like that of other old New England families. Their father guided them with strong Puritan values. Their mother was loving and nurturing. As a boy, Lawrence did his share of chores, including haying, planting, wood splitting and other farm work. However, he often found time to delight in the pleasures of childhood. He spent his free time playing in the woods and along the banks of the Penobscot River. He also enjoyed hiking and sailing.

Chamberlain experienced a great difficulty in his childhood which plagued him into adulthood. In his autobiography written much later in life, he described the particular malady as, "One of the miseries of his life." A speech impediment caused him to stammer when he tried to

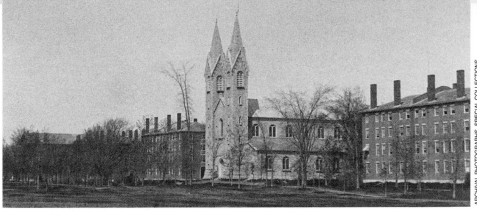

Bowdoin College Campus in 1855

speak words that began with the letters *p*, *b* and *t*. "It was," he later remembered, "at times impossible to get off a word beginning with one of those letters." This problem greatly disturbed him and, he later surmised, affected his entire life and character.

As a young boy, Chamberlain learned to overcome the problem. He taught himself a breathing pattern which he put into action when the letters approached. He "sang" his way past them. "But in truth," he remembered, "the sleepless anxiety on this score was a serious wear upon the nervous system. It was not much short of agonizing....This positive disability added to a natural timidity of self-assertion, apt to disclose itself on untimely occasions in that stupidity called bashfulness, had a decided effect on habits both of speech and action, which placed one at a serious disadvantage."

Growing up bashful, timid and stammering hardly limited him, though. By the time he grew to manhood, he decided he should attend college. The nearest school was one hundred miles down the Maine coast. To be admitted, however, he needed tutoring in order to meet the institute's strict entrance requirements. With typical Puritan persistence, he spent each day studying. He withdrew to the family attic from early in the morning to late at night. His only break from this rigorous schedule came when he walked more than a mile to Bangor to recite his lessons with a local teacher.

Bowdoin Days

He was soon ready for college. He traveled to Brunswick and entered Bowdoin College in 1848. Over the next four years, his life blossomed under a myriad of new experiences. The demanding college curriculum in those days involved the study of classics,

Joshua L. Chamberlain monument in Chamberlain Freedom Park, Brewer, Maine.

COLONEL JOHN BREWER LEFT the security of Worcester, Massachusetts in 1770 to explore the northern edges of the colony. At that time, Maine was not incorporated. He came upon the Penobscot River area and settled along the Sedgeunkedunk Stream. He named his discovery New Worcester. By 1788, the area, which included Brewer, Holden and Orrington, was incorporated as a town and re-named Orrington. The region developed as people ventured away from the established cities and towns in order to discover new

riches and land. Soon, Orrington grew into a large town and needed to be scaled down. In 1812, the community of Brewer received its present boundaries when it broke from Orrington and Holden broke from it. Brewer was incorporated as a city in 1889.

Brewer was a young town when Joshua L. Chamberlain was born in 1828. Not many houses or farms dotted the landscape. In fact, the Chamberlains had only eight or nine neighbors. However, the land was ripe with potential. As the years passed, people from all over the world settled in the area searching for a better life.

As Chamberlain matured, so, too, did Brewer. Coastal Maine grew tremendously during the 1800's. Rich caches of lumber attracted many people to Bangor and the Penobscot River area. Being close to both, Brewer also enjoyed prosperity.

Brewer's economy always depended on bricks and lumber. At one time, no less than twenty brickyards operated in the town. However, the easy-to-navigate waters of the Penobscot River and the power it generated attracted many other industries to the area. An early nineteenth century newspaper described them:

Among the lesser but still important industries in Brewer are the manufacturing of sails, boats, leather, wooden boxes, carriages, boots and shoes, brush woods, broom handles, churns, spinning wheels, woolen mittens, cooperage, harness, etc., and the usual trades and professions are represented in large number.

Brewer changed with each new enterprise. The population grew from 734 in 1820 to 4,835 eighty years later. The town no longer resembled the peaceful Eden discovered by the earlier explorers.

Across the Penobscot River, Bangor exploited the "lumber boom" of the 1800's. Many made and lost fortunes. Before long, it became the financial and commercial center of the region. By 1900, Bangor's population had grown to 21,850. Brewer's, on the other hand, stagnated. In fact, people largely ignored its riches until later in the century.

By the end of the twentieth century, Brewer experienced a rebirth. A bridge, built on the Penobscot River in 1954, made commuting between Brewer and Bangor easier. Desirable tracts of land attracted real estate developers, a variety of industries and commercial businesses. Brewer continues to become one of the fastest growing cities in the region.

rhetoric and theology. Students were required to read and recite numerous foreign languages. Despite his speech impediment, Lawrence mastered them all.

Among his most memorable experiences at Bowdoin probably included the handful of "Saturday Evenings" spent at the home of one of his professors. Dr. Calvin Stowe enjoyed informal discussion with his students and often invited them to his home. One evening, Professor Stowe's wife, Harriet Beecher Stowe, announced a special surprise. She was writing a story about slavery in Kentucky and wanted the students' opinions. She called her book *Life Among the Lowly*. Over the next few Saturdays, she read her manuscript aloud and discussed it with them. Little did they know that this quaint story would soon be published as *Uncle Tom's Cabin* and become one of the best selling books of all time.

THE SCHLESINGER LIBRARY, RADCLIFFE COLLEGE

Harriet Beecher Stowe, 1852

Frances Caroline "Fanny" Chamberlain, 1862

BOTH PHOTOS COURTESY OF THE PEJEPSCOT HISTORICAL SOCIETY

Joshua L. Chamberlain, c. 1858

Chamberlain met his future wife during those early days at Bowdoin. He conducted the choir at the First Parish Church. The pastor's young niece, Frances Caroline Adams, a distant cousin of former president John Quincy Adams, played the organ for the choir. "Fanny," as her friends called her, soon became Chamberlain's first love. As the years passed, their love matured and they spoke regularly of marriage.

Around that time, Chamberlain decided to change his name. Up until then, his friends called him "Jack," while his family called him "Lawrence." He decided to switch the first name with the middle. He now formally signed himself, "Joshua Lawrence Chamberlain."

By 1852, despite a leave-of-absence due to a lingering fever, Chamberlain finished his

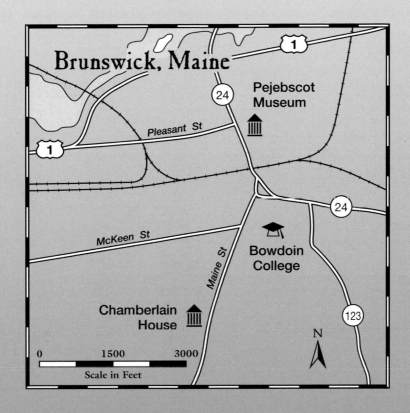

Brunswick, Maine

US 1

24

Pejebscot
Museum

Pleasant St

US 1

24

McKeen St

Maine St

Bowdoin
College

123

Chamberlain
House

N

0   1500   3000
Scale in Feet

Brunswick, along with many other coastal Maine towns, enjoyed great prosperity during the lumber boom of the early 19th century. The town was incorporated in 1739 and soon flourished. Its proximity to the Atlantic Ocean and the Androscoggin Falls created a solid foundation for lumbering, shipping, fishing and other industries. The town's historical district includes Bowdoin College and Joshua Chamberlain's home.

BOWDOIN COLLEGE CHANGED Joshua Chamberlain's life. It was the perfect environment for his growth. Within its walls he met and conquered many challenges. He rid himself of a debilitating stammer, became fluent in a variety of languages and discovered a gift for leadership.

Established in 1794, the small college named for Governor James Bowdoin, attracted some of the best minds in the country. The first students arrived in September 1802. Only one faculty member greeted them. But, the school's ideals were firmly established—and firmly communicated to these students. Joseph McKeen, the school's first president, admonished the students to use their education for the betterment of society. Over the years, most of the students heeded his words. By the 1820's, the school graduated an impressive number of alumni destined for greatness.

Franklin Pierce, the fourteenth president of the United States, graduated in 1824. Nathaniel Hawthorne and Henry Wadsworth Longfellow, two future literary giants, followed the next year. John Brown Russwurm, co-founder and co-editor of the country's first black

PHOTO BY DEAN ABRAMSON

Massachusetts Hall, Bowdoin College, completed in 1802. The college's oldest building.

newspaper, *Freedom's Journal*, became the college's first African American graduate in 1826.

Many Bowdoin graduates fought in the Civil War. At the time, the college reported that a larger percentage of its graduates fought for the Union than that of other schools. Oliver Otis Howard, class of 1850, was one of them. He sacrificed himself for the Union during the Battle of Seven Pines when he lost his arm. However, this did not end his military career, as he continued to serve his country throughout the remainder of the war. After the war, he headed the Freedmen's Bureau and founded Howard University. He served as its first president.

Governor John A. Andrews of Massachusetts, class of 1837, aided the war effort by bringing his state to a high degree of preparedness. He also formed the famous 54th Massachusetts regiment of black soldiers.

Joshua Chamberlain enrolled in 1848, and before long became one of the best students in his class. After graduation, he married Fanny Adams and joined the Bowdoin College staff as a junior instructor. By 1862 Chamberlain was a full professor of rhetoric. However, his nation needed strong, honorable men to fight the Confederate enemy, and he knew he had to help his country. He joined the 20th Maine and soon distinguished himself on the Civil War battlefields, earned a Congressional Medal of Honor and rose to the rank of brevet major general. When the war ended, he returned to Maine, served as its governor and continued a career at Bowdoin College. He served as president of the college from 1871 until 1883.

Robert E. Peary graduated in 1877. By 1909 he led the first expedition to the North Pole. When he returned to the United States, he received a promotion to rear admiral of the navy and became a national hero. One of his assistants, Donald B. MacMillan, class of 1898, led twenty-four additional expeditions to the Arctic. He enlisted Bowdoin College students as assistants.

Other famous Bowdoin College graduates include Alfred C. Kinsey, class of 1916. His research into human sexual behavior is still considered significant. In 1984, Joan Benoit Samuelson, class of 1979, won the first women's Olympic marathon.

View of United States Military Academy and the new Barracks, c. 1853.

studies. At the annual commencement, he received the honor of "first rank." This required him to give a speech. He later remembered that he suffered great nervousness during his oration because of the presence of his family and friends in the audience. Of course, the various dignitaries in the audience did not lessen the pressure. Many prominent graduates accepted the invitation to attend the ceremony that year because it was the school's fiftieth anniversary. As a result,

Chamberlain gave his speech in front of a large assembly, which included Henry Wadsworth Longfellow, Nathaniel Hawthorne and President-elect Franklin Pierce.

Bashfulness and his old stammering problem returned during the speech. By his own assessment, he failed miserably. Chamberlain was relieved when he finished. He just wanted to return to Brewer with his family.

Once Chamberlain graduated, he had to decide his future. Both parents had different ideas about which course he should choose. His father wanted him to attend West Point, while his mother wanted him to enter a seminary.

"My father," he recalled, "preferred I should pursue a military career, that being a manly and honorable path. As for my mother, however, she preferred the ministry for it was the Lord's own service; and whatever might befall, one would be sure he was faced the right way. I was not much inclined to either course for the reason that both alike afforded but little scope and freedom."

After much thought, Chamberlain chose his mother's hoped-for path. "In time, I decided that perhaps I could pursue the ministry wherein I could become a missionary to some really heathen country such as Africa, the Pacific islands or some other adventuresome destination."

Once he returned to Brewer, he entered Bangor Theological Seminary. Three years of intense study followed. At the

Maine Hall, Bangor Theological Seminary

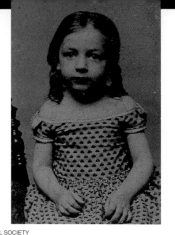

Grace Dupee Chamberlain,
c. 1862

Harold Wyllys Chamberlain,
c. 1862

Horace "Hod" Chamberlain

Joshua L. Chamberlain, 1860 Class Album, Bowdoin College

same time, Fanny, even though she accepted Joshua's proposal of marriage, decided to teach in Milledgeville, Georgia. When she left, Chamberlain focused almost exclusively on the completion of his training. He did not forget his beloved Fanny, though. He took time to write dozens of letters to her. They married in 1856.

Joshua and Fanny settled into a comfortable life. They purchased a house just beyond the main street from Bowdoin College. Two children, Grace Dupee (or Daisy) and Harold Wyllys, brought them abundant joy. In 1855, Chamberlain's old mentor, Professor Stowe, departed Bowdoin College. As a result, two positions opened: instructor of logical and natural theology and instructor of freshman Greek. The school decided to offer them to Chamberlain. The following year, his colleagues elected him professor of rhetoric and oratory. At this he marveled. Not only was the position prestigious for one so young, but it was an irony that a boy with a speech impediment could grow into a master of several languages and professor of oratory. Before long, he taught Spanish,

German, and the old Norse language to Bowdoin's students, which included his brothers John and Horace.

Chamberlain's life had moments of grief. Two of his four children died in infancy. His brother Horace, a promising lawyer, died of consumption (now called tuberculosis). Fanny lost most of her immediate family to disease, including her elderly parents. By 1861, Chamberlain longed for a change.

THE REMARKABLE STORY OF Joshua L. Chamberlain's life is preserved within the walls of the building he once called home. The Joshua L. Chamberlain Museum in Brunswick, Maine houses one of the finest collections of artifacts pertaining to Chamberlain, his family and his life.

The museum is operated by the Pejepscot Historical Society. The society, dedicated to conserving the history of the Pejepscot region of coastal Maine, believes that the Joshua L. Chamberlain House is important to its mission. It did not hesitate to save the house from demolition in 1983.

The front of the house is a comprehensive museum. Many relics are on display to help visitors understand Chamberlain. Other sections of the house are restored and open to the public.

History of the Joshua L. Chamberlain House

The house, in the shadows of Bowdoin College, was a natural choice for Professor Chamberlain. Before he assumed the house's mortgage and ownership in 1859 for $2,100, it passed through a succession of owners. Records are unclear as to who originally built the house. The common belief is that Captain Jesse Pierce constructed it and lived in it until he lost it to creditors in 1829. Mary Ann Fales then purchased it in 1830. She rented rooms, including three to the famous poet Henry Wadsworth Longfellow. By the time the Chamberlains moved in, six others claimed previous ownership.

Chamberlain enjoyed his new home. He spent many happy hours tending to its care and delighted in landscaping the garden. When he left to fight in the Civil War, he left detailed instructions on the winterization of the yard and the house.

After the war, Chamberlain returned to his life in Brunswick. As the years passed, he and Fanny renovated the "cape." They added many dramatic features. The chimneys were redesigned to feature a red Maltese cross, a Latin cross and a Greek cross. The roofline was extended to the southeast to cover a small side porch. They even moved the house to its present location on the corner of Maine and Potter streets.

While president of Bowdoin College, Chamberlain raised the first floor

Joshua L. Chamberlain Museum, Brunswick, Maine

and built a new bottom floor. He added a great entrance hall, a library, an office, a large dining room and drawing room. The new top floor accommodated his family's living quarters and guest rooms.

In 1900 Chamberlain chose to move to Portland and assume the duties of the Surveyor of the Port of Portland. Fanny died in 1905, but he remained in Portland until his death in 1914 at the age of eighty-five. He never sold the Brunswick house.

Upon his death, his daughter Grace inherited the house and its contents. She began renting out rooms in 1916. When she died in 1937, she willed the house to her daughter Rosamond. She sold it and its

contents to Emery Booker in 1939, who divided it into apartments. Years of neglect followed. Demolition seemed certain until the Pejepscot Historical Society purchased the structure in 1983.

For More Information
The Joshua L. Chamberlain Museum is located at 226 Maine Street, Brunswick, Maine 04011.

The Pejepscot Museum, located at 159 Park Row, Brunswick, Maine 04011, contains a large collection of Joshua L. Chamberlain research materials.

The web address for the Pejepscot Historical Society is www.curtislibrary.com/pejepscot/

WARRIOR

Joshua L. Chamberlain's house in Brunswick, Maine, before he added a new first floor.

DESPITE CHAMBERLAIN'S ENORMOUS SUCCESS at Bowdoin and contentment at home, he found his work dull. His earlier desire for adventure returned when the country collapsed into Civil War. Even if he wanted to, he probably had a difficult time putting thoughts of the conflict out of his mind. The sounds of fresh recruits practicing their military drills echoed in nearly every Maine town. As autumn

professor

pproached, Chamberlain resolved his feelings on the war. "The flag of the nation had been

sulted," he later wrote. "The honor and authority of the Union had been assaulted in

pen and bitter war. The north [sic] was at last awake to the intent and the magnitude of

e Rebellion. The country was roused to the peril and the duty of the hour."

C HAMBERLAIN WATCHED
the first campaigns of the war with
growing interest. He felt, as many did,
that each battle would be the last.
However, by the spring of 1862, it
became clear that the war would not end
quickly. The idea of military service,
dismissed as foolish in peacetime, grew
until it became an "irresistible impulse."
That same spring the college named him
professor of modern languages for life.
The position included a $500 bonus
and a leave-of-absence for two years in
order to travel to Europe. Once again he
felt honored, but the war proved to be
an immense distraction.

Governor Israel Washburne

Quietly, Chamberlain drafted a letter to
the governor of Maine explaining his
desire to join the war. The governor did
not take his offer lightly. Although many
Bowdoin men had already gone to the
seat of war as officers, Chamberlain was a
professor, a prized treasure of intellect.
Communities could not risk such assets
easily. The governor preferred he
remained where he was most needed to
ensure the future of his state and country.

Chamberlain understood this, but
argued the point in his correspondence
to the governor. "I fear, this war, so
costly of blood and treasure, will not
cease until men of the North are willing
to leave good positions, and sacrifice the
dearest personal interests, to rescue our

Major General Oliver Otis Howard

country from desolation, and defend the
national existence against treachery."

The argument convinced the governor.
He summoned Chamberlain to the
capital, and offered him command of
the next unit that was raised. Flattered
by the offer, but realizing the
responsibility, he declined. He offered to
serve in some lesser role so he could,
"learn the business first." Although he
was a master at languages and oratory,

he was far from prepared to fight in a war. He needed the more essential tools of a military officer. Not even the most eloquently styled argument, whether in German or Spanish, could win a battle once the bullets and shells parted the air. Dismissing this shortcoming, he wrote, "I have always been interested in military matters, and what I do not know in that line, I know how to learn."

Events moved swiftly. Another Bowdoin graduate, Major General Oliver Otis Howard, was in Brunswick recuperating from the loss of an arm during an earlier battle. Chamberlain privately sought his advice. The next day he learned that the local newspaper had misinterpreted his visit and proclaimed that he had accepted the colonelcy of the 20th Maine Regiment. Thus exposed, he was forced to deal with the Bowdoin trustees and faculty.

A delicate political balance governed the college. Two opposing religions maintained a fairly equal influence. Chamberlain remained firmly in the middle. Both sides feared that should he not return from the war, then his vacancy would undoubtedly shift the balance to either side. Fearing this, neither faction wanted him to leave.

They collaborated and sent a representative to discuss the matter with the governor. It is believed that they also encouraged a prominent Portland businessman to send a letter to the governor stating, "You have been deceived...he is nothing at all." However, letters from distinguished friends in Brunswick convinced the governor to dismiss the attacks. On August 8, 1862 Governor Israel Washburne appointed Chamberlain lieutenant colonel of the newly organized 20th Maine Regiment of Infantry. His Bowdoin colleagues reluctantly agreed to let him go.

The 20th Maine

The 20th Maine was about as far from an effective military unit as a mob could get. Many of the 1,000 men who gathered across from Portland at Camp Mason were misfits or miscreants. Only a few were Bowdoin men. The officers knew that the task of transforming them into well-trained soldiers would not be easy. However, the commander of the new

NATIONAL ARCHIVES

Colonel Adelbert Ames

Mustered In: August 29, 1862
Mustered Out: July 16, 1865
Enrollment: 1,621
Casualties: 147 killed or died of wounds; 381 wounded; 146 died of disease;
15 prisoners of war

Battle Site	Date
Antietam, Maryland	September 17, 1862
Shepherdstown Ford, Virginia	September 19-20, 1862
Fredericksburg, Virginia	December 13, 1862
Chancellorsville, Virginia.	May 1-4, 1863
Middleburg, Virginia.	June 17, 1863
Gettysburg, Pennsylvania	July 1-3, 1863
Rappahannock Station, Virginia	November 7, 1863
Mine Run, Virginia	November 26-December 1, 1863
Wilderness, Virginia	May 5-7, 1864
Spotsylvania, Virginia	May 7-20, 1864
North Anna, Virginia	May 23-27, 1864
Totopotomy, Virginia	May 26-30, 1864
Bethesda Church, Virginia	May 30-June 1, 1864
Cold Harbor, Virginia	May 31-June 12, 1864
Siege of Petersburg, Virginia	June 9, 1864-April 2, 1865
Jerusalem Plank Road, Virginia	June 22-23, 1864
Weldon Railroad, Virginia	August 18-21, 1864
Peebles Farm, Virginia	September 30-October 2, 1864
Hatcher's Run, Virginia	December 8-9, 1864
Quaker Road, Virginia	March 29, 1865
Gravely Run, Virginia	March 29, 1865
Five Forks, Virginia	March 30-April 1, 1865
Appomattox, Virginia	April 2-April 9, 1865

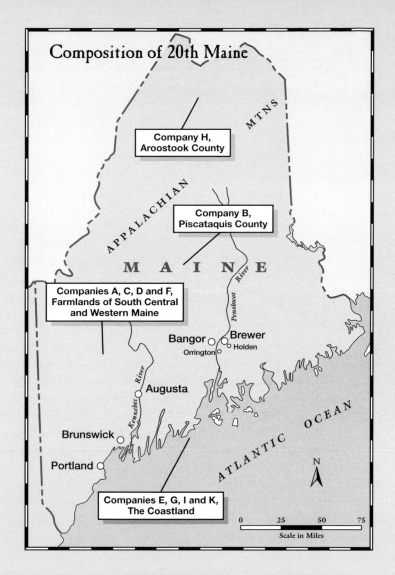

Composition of 20th Maine

Company H,
Aroostook County

Company B,
Piscataquis County

MAINE

Companies A, C, D and F,
Farmlands of South Central
and Western Maine

APPALACHIAN

MTNS

Penobscot River

Bangor   Brewer
   Orrington   Holden

Kennebec River

Augusta

Brunswick

Portland

ATLANTIC OCEAN

N

Companies E, G, I and K,
The Coastland

0   25   50   75
Scale in Miles

Maine was far from the Civil War battlefields. However, when the state issued a call to arms in 1862, men from four counties flocked to Portland to offer their strength and skills. On August 29, 1862 the 20th Maine was mustered in for service to the United States. By the war's end, the regiment earned a reputation for heroism and courage.

20th Maine Infantry regimental flag, retired after the Battle of Gettysburg, 1863.

regiment was perfect for the job. Colonel Adelbert Ames hailed from Rockland, Maine. He went to West Point and had already experienced fighting in the war. He was recuperating from a wound he received at the first Battle of Bull Run when he learned of his new command. He later earned a Medal of Honor for his actions at Bull Run, but he came home to Maine with a clean slate. He would not rest on past laurels.

Chamberlain arrived at the camp atop a most splendid horse. Upon hearing that he had sacrificed the comforts of home in order to defend their state, some prominent citizens of Portland collected money to bestow on him a beautiful dapple-gray horse. He was touched by the noble, well-meaning gift. He named his new companion "Prince." However, the gift was ill-chosen. The tall, light-colored horse presented a conspicuous target on the battlefield.

Chamberlain was ready to "learn the business." However, before he could assume his official position, a brief illness sent him home to Brunswick for a rest. The delay gave Fanny and a friend time to sew gold fringe on the regiment's new battle flag. Eventually, Chamberlain and the rest of the 20th Maine were ready to depart for the battlefields. Joshua and Fanny spent a final night together in a rain-soaked tent. Undoubtedly the presence of her adoptive father, the Reverend George Adams, in their shelter dampened the spirit of what could have been Chamberlain's last good-bye to her.

Colonel Ames arrived by the time the trains pulled out of camp on September 2. He immediately made his intentions for the unit known. Those intentions did not please the men. Ames had a reputation for being a strict disciplinarian. He grew up as a cabin boy on his father's sailing ships. He believed harsh punishment was necessary in order to maintain order. His years at West Point only sharpened his natural instincts, and he turned his will loose on the New England men. Up to this point, they had not accomplished a task as a group without first taking a vote. That was about to change.

Ames had experienced combat up close. He understood the need for discipline and physical stamina. They were

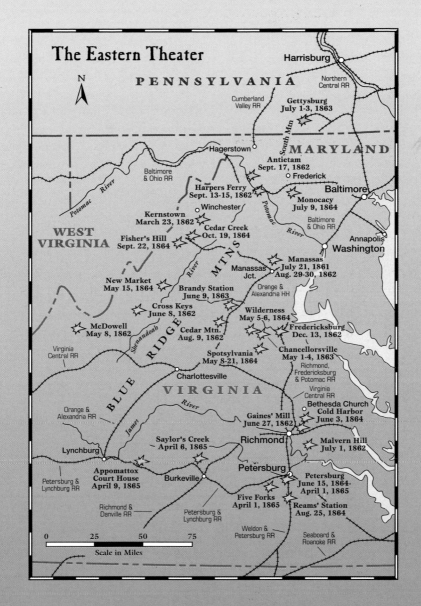

The Eastern Theater

N

PENNSYLVANIA

Harrisburg

Northern
Central RR

Cumberland
Valley RR

Gettysburg
July 1-3, 1863

South Mtn

MARYLAND

Hagerstown

Antietam
Sept. 17, 1862

Frederick

Baltimore
& Ohio RR

Potomac River

Harpers Ferry
Sept. 13-15, 1862

Winchester

Baltimore

Monocacy
July 9, 1864

Potomac River

Baltimore
& Ohio RR

**WEST
VIRGINIA**

Kernstown
March 23, 1862

Cedar Creek
Oct. 19, 1864

Fisher's Hill
Sept. 22, 1864

Annapolis
Washington

River

MTNS

Manassas
Jct.

Manassas
July 21, 1861
Aug. 29-30, 1862

New Market
May 15, 1864

Brandy Station
June 9, 1863

Orange &
Alexandria RR

Cross Keys
June 8, 1862

Wilderness
May 5-6, 1864

McDowell
May 8, 1862

Shenandoah River

BLUE

Cedar Mtn.
Aug. 9, 1862

Fredericksburg
Dec. 13, 1862

Virginia
Central RR

RIDGE

Spotsylvania
May 8-21, 1864

Chancellorsville
May 1-4, 1863

Richmond,
Fredericksburg
& Potomac RR

Charlottesville

VIRGINIA

Virginia
Central RR

Orange &
Alexandria RR

James River

Bethesda Church
Cold Harbor
June 3, 1864

Lynchburg

Saylor's Creek
April 6, 1865

Gaines' Mill
June 27, 1862

Richmond

Malvern Hill
July 1, 1862

Appomattox
Court House
April 9, 1865

Petersburg &
Lynchburg RR

Burkeville

Petersburg

Petersburg
June 15, 1864-
April 1, 1865

Richmond &
Danville RR

Petersburg &
Lynchburg RR

Five Forks
April 1, 1865

Reams' Station
Aug. 25, 1864

Weldon &
Petersburg RR

Seaboard &
Roanoke RR

0   25   50   75

Scale in Miles

The Eastern Theater area endured many of the Civil War's major battles. Virginia, in particular, suffered much of the hardship and destruction.

A T THE AUGUST 29-30, 1862 Second Battle of Bull Run in Virginia, General Robert E. Lee's Army of Northern Virginia drove Major General John Pope's Union army towards Washington, D. C. Lee, with his opponents reeling, took the opportunity to move northward into Maryland. This movement threatened the Northern capital. It also took both armies away from the food crops being harvested in Virginia.

Major General George McClellan, the commander of the Army of the Potomac, cautiously followed Lee. He finally caught up with him near Sharpsburg, Maryland. Before he arrived, he received a tremendous gift from two Indiana soldiers who found a copy of Lee's plans.

At daybreak on September 17, Major General Joseph Hooker's First Corps advanced. Vicious fighting resulted. By the end of the day, 23,000 men were counted as either dead, wounded or captured. The bloodshed shocked both sides. The battle was considered inconclusive, yet Lee chose to withdraw.

Three days later, as the Union troops advanced on the retreating Confederates, some of Lee's men fought a rearguard action at Shepherdstown Ford on the

NATIONAL PARK SERVICE

Dunker Church, used by the pacifist German Baptist Brethren, was the site of intense fighting on September 14, 1862.

Potomac River. The fighting did not last long and they soon retreated. McClellan had stopped Lee's first invasion of the North.

Chamberlain at the Battles of Antietam and Shepherdstown Ford

Chamberlain and the 20th Maine received their first lessons on the brutality of war on the battlefields of Antietam and Shepherdstown Ford. Just formed, barely trained, they stayed on the edges of the fray. What they saw began to harden them to the realities of war.

The 20th Maine entered the race towards Maryland on September 12. The march was brutal. Only a small portion of the regiment completed the first sixteen miles from Washington, D.C. Stragglers caught up that night, only to be forced into a twenty-four mile hike the next day. On September 14, they arrived at South Mountain.

Chamberlain watched the Union troops move up to the Sharpsburg Road. He stood looking westward from Turner's Gap over the valley of the Antietam Creek. Beyond, the Confederate forces marched to higher ground, between the Antietam Creek and Sharpsburg, Maryland.

On September 16, as both sides filed into line, the 20th Maine, as part of the Fifth Army Corps, remained in reserve. It bivouacked just beyond the village of Keedysville, behind the center of the Federal line.

The next day, during the harsh battle, Chamberlain and a few of the other officers climbed to the top of a hill to watch the battle as it unfolded in Miller's cornfield. Later that morning, they received orders to move a few hundred yards to the south in order to protect the army wagon trains, the reserve artillery and the batteries overlooking the center bridge. The men from Maine did not taste their first fighting until three days later, at Shepherdstown Ford.

The regiment crossed the Potomac River on September 20 in order to obtain a better view of the retreating Confederates. Lee's men needed to create a delaying action, so they turned and offered battle at Shepherdstown Ford. The 20th Maine, crossing the Potomac River at that moment, came under Confederate fire for the first time. A few minutes later the buglers sounded retreat and the men backed down a bluff and recrossed the river under more fire. For the next few days the 20th Maine

LIBRARY OF CONGRESS

Into the Cornfield *sketched by Alfred R. Waud, September 17, 1862.*

tangled with Confederate sharpshooters hiding in the ruins of an old mill on the Virginia (now West Virginia) side of the river. Eventually, Union artillery flushed the snipers from the rubble and drove them deeper into Virginia.

Points of Interest at Antietam National Battlefield

Prye House, McClellan's Headquarters - Near the spot where Chamberlain and the 20th Maine glimpsed their first sights of battle.

Shepherdstown Ford - Site where the 20th Maine experienced fighting for the first time. Travel south on Maryland 65 towards Sharpsburg.

Turn right at stop sign onto Maryland 34 west. Turn left at stop sign in Shepherdstown onto German Street. Follow it as it bends to the Potomac River. Becomes River Road. Ruins of the old mill are on the left.

Information About the Park

Antietam National Battlefield is on Route 65, north of Sharpsburg. To learn more about the battle or the site, contact the park.

Antietam National Battlefield
PO Box 158
Sharpsburg, Maryland 21782-0158

Web Address: www.nps.gov/anti/

essential if one was to endure long marches and fierce battles. The newly assembled group did not appreciate his benevolent intentions. They hated him for his strictness and feared his punishments. Ames did not take their resentment to heart, though. For the moment, he accepted those emotions as sufficient.

The 20th Maine made its way by train and steamship to Boston, then to Washington, D.C. There it was assigned to the Fifth Corps of the Army of the Potomac. Before long, word came that the Confederate army had invaded Maryland. A brutal march westward immediately took the new regiment to its first battle. Ames could not have devised a better test for his command. By the time the 20th Maine reached the scene of the war, so many men had fallen out with sore feet and tired legs,

that it could hardly be called a unit.

Battle of Antietam

The ragamuffin lot reorganized in time to be in line during the Battle of Antietam, the bloodiest single day in American military history. To its utter good fortune, the Fifth Corps was held out of the battle. From a hillside high above the spot where the Antietam Bridge carries the Boonsboro Pike over Antietam Creek, and not far from army headquarters, some of the men caught a brief glimpse of the distant battle.

After a day of intense fighting and a day of truce, the Confederates retreated. The 20th Maine received its first taste of battle while pursuing them from the battlefield. At a Potomac River crossing called Shepherdstown Ford, the new regiment stumbled across the shallow point of the river,

Antietam Bridge on the Sharpsburg-Boonsboro Turnpike. Wartime photograph taken by Alexander Gardner.

Unknown Union unit performing drills.

exchanged a few bullets with a largely unseen enemy on the heights beyond, and then fell back to the previous shoreline. Chamberlain conducted himself well during his first brush with war. He sat calmly upright in the saddle of a horse borrowed from Major Gilmore of the regiment and encouraged his men from the middle of the river. He remained in the water until the horse beneath him was shot in the head. This was the first of six times a horse bearing him would be struck in battle.

For weeks after this brief encounter with the enemy, the regiment camped in unsanitary conditions without tents or proper food. Many of the men, not accustomed to crowding together with hundreds of others, became sick. A few even died of disease. However, Ames did not soften his approach. He had a

singular determination to prepare his men for the next encounter with the enemy. Day after day, he relentlessly pushed his men to practice their drills and maneuvers.

Ames knew that it was critical for the men to learn to react instinctively in battle. Nothing assured that more than incessant drilling. Hour upon hour of repetition would help the men endure the smoke, the panic and the confusion of a battle. The men had to act exactly as ordered. Ames had little time to prepare them. By his experience, he knew that he had to be unforgiving in his approach. As a result, the men's ability to perform grew at a pace equal to their hatred of him.

In a letter home to his family in Brewer, Tom Chamberlain, now a sergeant in one of the 20th Maine's ten companies, relayed the feelings of many, "I tell you he is as savage a man you ever saw," he wrote. "I swear the men will shoot him the first battle we are in." What Tom Chamberlain failed to realize was that Ames was bringing out the soldier in him. In the same letter, he added, "If I can't knock Frank Sabine drilling I will give it up." Despite the hatred, the men were learning their task.

The depth of the men's hostility towards Ames matched their admiration for Chamberlain. Chamberlain chose to be less rigid than Ames. "Our lieutenant colonel is one of the finest men that ever lived," one private declared. Another said, "He is full of military, brave but considerate and treats the men like men not dogs."

As intent as ever to "learn the business first," he focused on his duty in the same way that he had his formal education. In a letter to Fanny, he wrote, "I study, I tell you, every military work I can find." He was determined to absorb as much of the military training as possible. By day, he observed his commanding officer. At night, he talked to him. The two huddled by candlelight over books and papers. They discussed strategies, tactics and events of the war.

Officers of the 20th Maine. From left to right: Ellis Spear, William Bickford, James Stanwood, Walter Morrill, William Morrell, Henry Sidelinger and Atherthon Clark. Taken at Rappahannock Station, Virginia in 1863. Chamberlain was home on sick leave when this photograph was taken.

Chamberlain, ever the scholar, wrote to Fanny requesting that she send him copies of various military texts. One might find it difficult to see how *The Art of War* by the Swiss general Antoine Henri Jomini could be of use to a lieutenant colonel of infantry. However, he approached problems by studying. He gave his new career his usual diligent effort.

The rest of the men struggled under Ames's harsh tutelage. With winter coming, they probably began to wonder if they would ever use their developing skills against the enemy. By the end of December's second week, however, it was clear they would soon have that chance.

earnest

Major General William B. Franklin's Union command crossed the Rappahannock River on a ponto

SIX WEEKS AFTER RETREATING FROM MARYLAND, the Confederate army established itself in a solid, fortified position atop a long, sloping hill that overlooked the small town of Fredericksburg, Virginia. The Union army camped not too far away. Ea of town ran the Rappahannock River. Across that river, on a bluff of their own, were Majo

ridge at this point near Fredericksburg, Virginia.

General Ambrose E. Burnside and the Army of the Potomac. Burnside wanted to hurry his

army toward the Confederate capital of Richmond. However, he could not achieve that

goal from his current position without leaving a hostile army in his rear. And that was out

of the military question.

BURNSIDE PROCRASTINATED, giving the enemy more time to fortify the heights it occupied. When he commenced the assault, disaster resulted. On December 13, 1862, Burnside commanded his men to attack the enemy position on the heights west of town. As ordered, regiment after regiment, brigade after brigade, crossed the river, passed through the town and marched up a long slope directly into heavy Confederate fire. Each successive wave of blue-clad troops marched toward the enemy, in plain view and without any cover. Each wave was slaughtered on the field.

LIBRARY OF CONGRESS

Major General Ambrose E. Burnside

As the sun began to set on the first day of this madness, the Fifth Corps, including the 20th Maine, received its orders to cross the river. Moving across a temporary pontoon bridge, the regiment entered the town. It turned right and marched up Hanover Street. From there, its route to the enemy's front line was over sloping farmland. Pausing to form his men for battle, Colonel Ames declared to Chamberlain, "This is earnest work. God help us now! Take care of the right wing...Forward!" As the line began to ascend, Ames walked calmly, fearlessly to the front. He ignored the bullets and cannonfire. Sheepish, but inspired, his men followed slowly.

Chamberlain, keeping both his book-learning and Ames's example in mind, advanced with his colonel. As he moved forward, he came upon a board fence which impeded his men's march up the slope. He quickly ordered his men to move it. With bullets whizzing past, Chamberlain turned back toward the right wing, shouting, "Do you want me to do it?" As one soldier reported, "Aid was immediately forthcoming, and the fence soon came down."

Lying on the ground further up the hill, a soldier from another regiment already on the scene, paused a moment to look to the rear. He beheld "...the

Marye's Heights, Fredericksburg, Virginia

20th Maine...coming across the field in line of battle, as upon parade, easily recognized by their new state colors...It was a grand sight, and a striking example of what discipline will do for such material in such a battle."

"Shortly after, a tall, slim colonel coolly walked over our bodies. 'Who commands this regiment,' he asked. Our colonel responded. 'I will move over your line and relieve your men,' he quietly rejoined. It was Colonel Adelbert Ames...We fell back through their lines a few yards. The 20th Maine swept forward...."

The 20th Maine reached its assigned position and immediately felt relief. The sun had set and darkness soon concealed the men. Also, the ground which they now occupied offered some protection. Though less than 300 yards from the enemy, previous regiments had made it safer by building crude breastworks of logs and boards. After an initial period of firing, during which the regiment

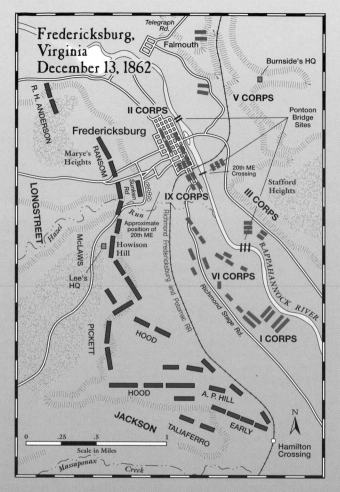

Fredericksburg,
Virginia
December 13, 1862

Telegraph Rd.

Falmouth

Burnside's HQ

V CORPS

Pontoon Bridge Sites

R. H. ANDERSON

II CORPS

Fredericksburg

RANSOM

Marye's Heights

Sunken Rd.

20th ME Crossing

Stafford Heights

LONGSTREET

McLAWS

IX CORPS

Run

Hazel

Approximate position of 20th ME

Howison Hill

Richmond Fredericksburg and Potomac RR

III CORPS

RAPPAHANNOCK RIVER

Lee's HQ

VI CORPS

Richmond Stage Rd.

PICKETT

HOOD

I CORPS

HOOD

A. P. HILL

EARLY

N

JACKSON

TALIAFERRO

Hamilton Crossing

0   .25   .5   1

Scale in Miles

Massaponax   Creek

Major Ambrose E. Burnside initially planned to quickly move through Fredericksburg in an effort to attack Richmond, Virginia. Instead, delays crossing the Rappahannock River allowed the Confederate army to position itself between the Union troops and Richmond. Burnside's effort to dislodge General Robert E. Lee's troops led to a tremendous defeat. At first, Chamberlain and the 20th Maine, attached to the Fifth Corps, remained in reserve at Stoneman's Switch, five miles north of Falmouth. They entered the battle when more men were needed for the assault on Marye's Heights. Finally on December 16, the Union forces left the battlefield and Chamberlain led his men to safety over the pontoon bridges on the Rappahannock River.

Colonel Ellis Spear of the 20th Maine

suffered few casualties, the men settled into their new place in line and made it as safe as possible before the sun rose again.

The 20th Maine Holds Its Position

The night was cold and offered little relief. The men began to realize that not only were they somewhat exposed to the enemy, but they were also largely cut off from the rest of the army. One soldier remembered, "consultation of officers was held in which most were of the opinion that it would be useless to try to hold the position...Colonel Ames, however, insisted that the ground must be held...so it was decided to hold the ground, and hold it we did."

Through the cold night and into the next morning, the entire brigade remained in its precarious position. The enemy first tried to shell the men out, then it sent a group of sharpshooters to drive them out with bullets. Through the day and again into the night, they held on while relief troops waited, unable to reach them across the open plain. As the sun went down, the cold returned. Lying on the ground just a few yards from the enemy, the men waited. Chamberlain felt the stinging December cold as much as his men. He had no blanket and with the adjutant of the regiment as his only companion, moved around as best he could in order to keep warm. He occasionally stopped to seek warmth under his winter coat. "I did sleep, though," he remembered a few days later. "Strange as you may think it, in the very midst of a heap of dead, close beside one dead man, touching him possibly."

Chamberlain pulled the flap of his coat over his head to conserve warmth. At one point in the night, some soldiers hoping to find survivors among the dead bodies, lifted the flap. Chamberlain opened his eyes. Startled by this response from what they presumed was a corpse, the soldiers gasped and hurried away. During this second night, orders arrived finally to withdraw. The 20th Maine

MAJOR GENERAL AMBROSE E. Burnside assumed the command of the Army of the Potomac from Major General George B. McClellan on November 7, 1862. By November 17 he had re-organized the army and marched to Stafford Heights, across from Fredericksburg, Virginia. Lee was surprised by the move, for he had not anticipated Burnside's quickness. Burnside, however, could not move any further south until he crossed the Rappahannock River. To do that, he needed pontoon bridges. The army bureaucracy, slow-moving and incompetent, conspired with the sloppy, cold weather to delay their arrival.

The delay allowed Lee to take control of the hills behind Fredericksburg and position men along the Rappahannock River. When the Union engineers finally obtained the pontoon boats and tried to build the pontoon bridges, a brigade from Mississippi, located in the town, made the task difficult by raining shot at and around them.

In retaliation, Burnside bombarded the town. The Mississippians reappeared from the rubble, and forced wave after wave of Union combat troops to ride across the river to drive them away. Once that task was accomplished, the Army of the Potomac began crossing the Rappahannock River.

NATIONAL PARK SERVICE

Chatham House, Union headquarters and field hospital during the Battle of Fredericksburg.

December 13 dawned cold and foggy. Both the Confederate and Union soldiers waited tensely for the battle to begin. Finally, Burnside issued his attack orders. Although some Union troops briefly captured a position held by a portion of "Stonewall" Jackson's corps, they were quickly driven back. Along the rest of the battle line, many Union troops were slaughtered as they crossed open ground against the Confederates on Marye's Heights and behind a stone wall. The fighting ended with the setting of the sun. Nothing was resolved.

Burnside wanted to try again the next day, but his men persuaded him not to order another assault. He recrossed the Rappahannock River and dismantled his pontoon bridges.

The Battle of Fredericksburg was a disaster for the Union. The Army of the Potomac suffered 12,700 casualties. Almost two-thirds of the Union loss occurred at the base of Marye's Heights. The Confederates suffered approximately 5,400 casualties.

Joshua L. Chamberlain at the Battle of Fredericksburg

The 20th Maine was attached to the Fifth Corps, part of Hooker's Center Grand Division. At first, the men remained in reserve at Stoneman's Switch, north of town. The wait was not easy. The weather was cruel, and during the night of December 6, two men froze to death.

Chamberlain witnessed the first assaults to take Marye's Heights from the north bank of the Rappahannock River. Charge after charge failed. When Burnside needed more men, the 20th Maine received its orders to advance.

Entering the fray with the First Division's Third Brigade, the men of the 20th Maine crossed to the Fredericksburg side of the river. Once there, the brigade reorganized in the lower part of the town. Chamberlain and his commander, Colonel Adelbert Ames, waited in the middle of a street for orders. Initially, other brigades moved forward. Finally, the 20th received word to advance. It had no choice but to cross over the bodies of fallen comrades. Fighting was intense, yet Marye's Heights was still a quarter mile distant. After an attempt at dusk, the 20th remained pinned down behind a low rise in the ground.

The next day, fighting resumed. The 20th Maine waited among the dead for its orders. In the afternoon, it moved to drive off a large party of the enemy from behind the wall at Marye's Heights. Chamberlain received a grazing from a minié ball.

After thirty-six hours of being on the frontline, the 20th finally moved to the shelter of town. That night, the men made camp along Caroline Street. The next day, some light skirmishing took place. Finally, on the 16th, Chamberlain led the regiment back across the pontoon bridges, to safety.

Points of Interest at Fredericksburg and Spotsylvania County National Military Park

Wolf Street Near Princess Anne Street - Spot where the 20th Maine was trapped during its advance to Marye's Heights.

Marye's Heights Walking Trail - Twice the focal point of Union attack. Over 15,000 men died in the Union's futile attempt to capture it.

National Cemetery Walking Trail - Located at Marye's Heights. Dedicated in July 1865 to the Union soldiers who are buried here.

Chatham House - Union headquarters and field hospital.

Information about the Park
Located fifty miles south of Washington, D.C. and fifty miles north of Richmond, Virginia. For more information about the battle and the site, contact the park.

Fredericksburg and Spotsylvania County National Military Park
120 Chatham Lane
Fredericksburg, Virginia 22405

Web Address: www.nps.gov/frsp/

Fredericksburg from the east bank of the Rappahannock River.

took with it its dead and wounded and moved toward the town below. The strange and disturbing glow of an Aurora Borealis, more commonly seen in Maine than in Virginia, lit the march.

"Fiery lances and banners of blood, and flame," Chamberlain recalled. "Columns of pearly light, garlands and wreaths of gold - all pointing and beckoning upward. Befitting scene! Who would die a nobler death, or dream of more glorious burial? Dead for their country's honor, and lighted to burial by the meteor splendors of their Northern home!"

The men buried their comrades, then moved down an unfinished railroad bed. They bivouacked in the town. "It was a sight worthy of the French Revolution," one of them remembered. "Bivouacs in the street, artillery moving up and down, and all the noise and confusion of an army."

Federal pontoon bridges on the Rappahannock River.

The 20th Maine spent December 14 and the following day recuperating. They finally attained much-needed rest. By midnight, however, new orders arrived. They had to march back to their abandoned position on the hill. Before long, they resumed their places in the old rifle pits with the knowledge that the enemy was waiting for first light to destroy them.

Temporary Command

The brigade's commander fell ill and Colonel Ames assumed temporary control. The regiment's leadership went to Chamberlain. His orders were simple and stark, but too common in army parlance for any soldier's liking, "Hold this ground at all hazards," it said. "And to the last."

Chamberlain did what he could to encourage the men. He walked along the line, keeping low and quiet. Near the end of what he perceived was his command, he saw a man throwing dirt out of his hole and down the slope. "Throw to the other side, man," he commanded. "That's where the danger is!" The reply shocked him. "Golly!" a decidedly Southern voice declared. "Don't ye s'pose I know which side them Yanks be?" Realizing his predicament and not wanting to expose his particular national loyalty, Chamberlain summoned his least Northern accent and replied, "Dig away then, but keep a right sharp lookout!" Then he stealthily retraced his steps.

He caught his breath, but was again forced to use his wits in order to keep the nearby enemy at bay. A Union staff officer rode up the hill asking for the regiment's commander and on encountering Chamberlain, cried out, "Get yourselves out of this as quick as God will let you! The whole army is across the river."

Chamberlain had to think fast. His new-found Rebel acquaintance (and any number of other brethren) undoubtedly caught the remark and its inviting opportunity. He called out loudly, "Steady in your places men!...arrest this stampeder! This is a ruse of the enemy." After a quieter apology from the bellowing officer, Chamberlain and Ames, aided by a cloud-covered moon and a prevailing wind, moved the men down the slope, through the town and across the river to safety. Chamberlain and the regiment had endured their first real brush with the horrors of war. If they had felt a thirst for combat before the battle, then it had been slaked on the slopes above Fredericksburg.

A TEST

Burnside's infamous Mud March *sketched by Alfred R. Waud.*

NOTHER DISASTROUS ACTION followed this failure of the overall Union effort to dislodge the Confederate army. Afterwards, it became known as the "Mud March." Burnside planned to maneuver around the enemy and to attack it by surprise. He stepped off on the preparatory march on January 20. The rain bega

of strength

y late afternoon and did not cease for three days. Several times it came down in

orrents, while the temperature warmed rapidly. The roads became an enormous

uagmire. The army stopped and did all that it could just to get out of the mud and

ack to its camps.

47

President Abraham Lincoln

Major General George McClellan

GENERAL BURNSIDE'S FUTURE was doomed. These setbacks contributed significantly to his departure. However, he was merely the latest commander of the Army of the Potomac. He had replaced Major General George McClellan, who had replaced Major General John Pope, who was not the first commander to lead the Union soldiers in little more than a year of warfare. President Lincoln knew the Union army needed someone to lead it out of confusion and to victory. He turned to Major General Joseph Hooker.

General Joseph Hooker took several months to move his army into a better position. He wanted the next confrontation with the Confederates to take place without the hindrance of a large sloping hill between them. A few miles west of the previous battlefield, he crossed the Rappahannock River and set up a defensive position on ground of his own choosing. He waited near a place called "Chancellor House." He believed that when the eventual battle erupted, his much larger army could flank and destroy the enemy. Unfortunately, when the Confederates made their move, he froze.

Small Pox Outbreak

The time arrived for Ames and Chamberlain to test the mettle of their men. They had trained them into the best possible condition and were anxious to show their comrades what they could do in a fight. Toward the last of April and into the first several days of May, 1863, their chance seemed at hand. Despite their best efforts, however, the

20th Maine sat out the fighting portion of what later became known as the Battle of Chancellorsville.

Before the two armies drew up across from one another, the 20th Maine supposedly received a vaccination against small-pox. A mistake at some point caused a live version of the disease to be substituted for, or at least mixed with, the vaccine. As a result, an enormous outbreak of the pox completely disabled the regiment for service. At least three men died and three dozen more were sent from the war to recover.

duty. He managed to obtain a temporary assignment on the staff of fellow Mainer, Major General Oliver Otis Howard, commander of the Union Eleventh Corps. Chamberlain, left in command of the regiment, tried his best to get his men into the fight. At one point, he argued that, "if we couldn't do anything else, we could at least give the enemy small pox." He could not convince his superiors of this new strategy of war, or to even put the 20th Maine into the fight.

Major General Joseph Hooker   Major General Oliver Otis Howard   Brigadier General Charles Griffin

Despite the protests of its commander, the 20th Maine was relegated to guarding the telegraphs at the rear. Colonel Ames, however, did not want to waste his time performing this

Chamberlain desperately wanted to join the battle. He finally got his wish when Brigadier General Charles Griffin sent word that he could advance toward the action with another brigade in the division. He would have done better to have stayed out of the battle. He received little experience and lost his dapple-gray "gift horse." At some point in the advance, a piece of shell struck Prince in the head, rendering him disabled from service.

General Robert E. Lee

Chamberlain Assumes Command

Chancellorsville became yet another defeat in a long and growing list of Union setbacks. The battle did much to elevate the Confederate commander General Robert E. Lee to mythical status. Although the Union troops outnumbered his army by three to one at many points on the field, he drove them from the area to a more northerly line of defense.

The army's situation continued to deteriorate. By June, searing heat added to its misery and depressed the already low morale. Just six months earlier, Union officials thought they had the Confederate army within its grasp. Now Lee and his men marched north toward Maryland, and beyond.

Adelbert Ames impressed General Howard at the Battle of Chancellorsville, and received a promotion to head one of his brigades. Chamberlain officially assumed command of the 20th Maine. But, by the third week of June he had to relinquish his new office. The heat, exhaustion and weeks of long, hard pursuit of the enemy had left him ill and weak. Doctors forced him into bed with what they termed "malarial fever." However, before he could rest, he had to diffuse a difficult, volatile situation.

During the last few days in May, army commanders assigned the men from the 2nd Maine to the 20th Maine. This regiment had been disbanded, as it had served its two year enlistment. However, about one hundred men, who had enlisted long after the regiment left for war, had time remaining to serve. Most of them took their place with the new regiment. However, about three score refused. They met Chamberlain under the bayonets of a neighboring regiment. The orders were clear and to the point.

General Thomas J. "Stonewall" Jackson, one of Lee's most trusted officers, died at the Battle of Chancellorsville when his own men mistook him for the enemy.

These men must serve or he could have them shot for desertion.

He could not do that. He knew he could never return to Maine if he shot some of its native sons. He had to discover another way to handle the problem. While many officers would have gruffly scolded the "mutineers," as they were called, Chamberlain tried a different tack.

These men had spent many days without rations. He ordered his own men to get them food. Then, realizing that the rough handling of anonymous army commanders had put them into their present state of mind, he talked directly

to them. He listened to their grievances. While promising no particular results, he showed sympathy. He also promised to write to the governor about their issues. At first, the men were hostile. But in time, all but two willingly, and many quite heroically, served under the 20th Maine's regimental flag.

Chamberlain Promoted

Now Chamberlain could rest. His brother John, visiting his brothers to experience their military lives, came at a most opportune time. Joshua became so ill that by June 21 his doctors ordered him to remain off duty while he recuperated. Tom, who was now the regimental adjutant, remained with the regiment, while John accompanied Joshua. The two brothers followed the army, but stopped at houses along the way. This strategy seemed to help Joshua regain his strength.

The 2nd Maine Volunteer Infantry on Christmas Day in 1861. Part of this regiment was transferred to the 20th Maine in May 1863.

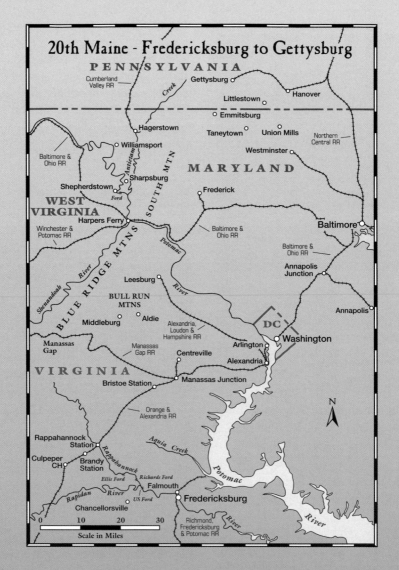

20th Maine - Fredericksburg to Gettysburg

PENNSYLVANIA

Cumberland
Valley RR

Creek

Gettysburg

Littlestown

Hanover

Emmitsburg

Taneytown   Union Mills

Northern
Central RR

Hagerstown

Williamsport

Westminster

MARYLAND

Baltimore &
Ohio RR

Antietam

SOUTH MTN

Sharpsburg

Shepherdstown

Frederick

WEST
VIRGINIA

Ford

Harpers Ferry

Baltimore
Ohio RR

Baltimore &
Ohio RR

Baltimore

Winchester &
Potomac RR

Potomac

Baltimore &
Ohio RR

Annapolis
Junction

BLUE RIDGE MTNS

River

Leesburg

River

Annapolis

Shenandoah

BULL RUN
MTNS

Middleburg   Aldie

Alexandria,
Loudon &
Hampshire RR

DC

Washington

Manassas
Gap

Manassas
Gap RR

Centreville

Arlington

Alexandria

VIRGINIA

Bristoe Station

Manassas Junction

N

Orange &
Alexandria RR

Rappahannock
Station

Aquia Creek

Culpeper
CH

Rappahannock

Potomac

Brandy
Station

Ellis Ford   Richards Ford

Rapidan   River

Falmouth

US Ford

Chancellorsville

Fredericksburg

River

0   10   20   30

Richmond,
Fredericksburg
& Potomac RR

Scale in Miles

After his crushing victories at Fredericksburg and Chancellorsville, General Robert E. Lee decided to invade the North. He headed for Pennsylvania. His idea to strike this area was significant, as he realized that by occupying it, he might be able to threaten Philadelphia, Baltimore and Washington, D.C. He believed the Confederacy would then receive recognition from Great Britain and France.

John Chamberlain

General James Longstreet

Chamberlain's recovery was slow. But, by June 30 it was obvious that the war's intensity was building to a crescendo that was about to erupt. Chamberlain could not stay away any longer. Although not fully recovered, he could not bear the idea of deserting his men as the fighting loomed. He returned to the regiment, near a place called Union Mills in Maryland. Here he discovered that he had been promoted to colonel.

Later that day, the Fifth Corps passed into Pennsylvania in pursuit of Lee and his men. The sounds of cannon echoed in the distance. The army, now under the command of Major General George Gordon Meade, prepared for an enormous battle. Chamberlain readied his men. The next day they set out on a fifteen mile march westward toward a small town called Gettysburg.

Generals of the Army of the Potomac at Culpeper, Virginia, 1863. Gouverneur K. Warren, William H. French, George Gordon Meade, Henry J. Hunt, Andrew A. Humphreys, John Sedgwick.

HOLD THIS PLACE

Little Round Top, Gettysburg, July, 1863. Big Round Top is seen in the background to the right.

EVEN BEFORE THE 20TH MAINE ARRIVED in Pennsylvania, it heard stories of the battle that had commenced about eighteen hours earlier. It discerned from

at all hazards

he rumor mill that the day had not gone well for the Union forces. Many began to

onder if yet another debacle awaited the Union.

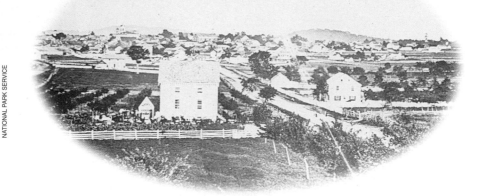

View of Gettysburg from Seminary Ridge shortly after the battle.

THE 20TH MAINE reached the hamlet of Gettysburg in the very early hours of July 2 and took its place in rear of the center of what became an arch-shaped Union battle line. By mid-afternoon, battle sounds could be heard off to the left end of the Union line, which had grown into the shape of a fishhook. The 20th Maine was assigned to the top of its shank. After hurrying a mile or so towards its assigned position, it halted at the edge of a wheat field and saw for the first time the surging Confederate assault. The regiment moved along, hurrying back around and up the rear of a prominent hill.

The three Chamberlain brothers rode abreast. Just as they turned for their new course, a shell exploded uncomfortably close by. A fragment of the shell struck the head of a horse in the regiment just behind them. Chamberlain felt the danger. He told his brothers, "Boys, I don't like this. Another such shot might make it hard for mother." He sent John ahead to help establish a place for the wounded. He sent Tom to the rear of the column to keep it moving. He led the regiment to its place in the line of battle: a wooded area, on a small rocky outcropping of a large hill.

Atop an obscure Pennsylvania hill on what became the most important day of his life, Joshua Chamberlain was anything but prepared for combat. He still suffered from weakness and fever. Moreover, he was still relatively inexperienced. He fought only once in battle with the regiment, and then under the supervision of Ames. He had good reason to be hesitant, but had to summon the strength to lead his men into combat.

His orders provided little guidance or comfort. After speaking with him for a moment, the brigade commander, Colonel Strong Vincent, pointed out to Chamberlain that his was the last regiment in the entire Union line. The commander closed with a terse instruction consisting of one sentence: "Hold this place at all hazards."

As the brigadier walked away, Chamberlain took stock of his difficult situation. His health was shaky. He and his regiment had little combat experience. His position was vulnerable. To his right, mostly obscured from view, were the other three regiments of the brigade. To his left, there was nothing but wooded and rocky Pennsylvania countryside. In military terms, his flank was "in the air." That meant his left was completely exposed to surprise attack.

His men built a crude shelter against ambush by piling up tree limbs with other debris. Within a few minutes, bullets began flying. Then the Confederates that were firing them came out of the woods. At first, they faced the 20th Maine's right wing at a fairly comfortable distance. But, Chamberlain soon discerned that more of the enemy

MOLLUS

Colonel Strong Vincent. He was promoted to brigadier general at the time of his death.

was moving towards his exposed left. He saw the direction of the movement and ordered the regiment to "refuse the line." He wanted them to extend themselves and bend back so that they formed the shape of a "V" on the crest of the hill. That way, the men on the right could keep firing at the enemy in front, while the men on the left bent back to meet any assault from that direction.

His plan was correct. Colonel William Oates, the man commanding the attacking Confederates and a veteran of nearly every prior major battle, watched as his men reached the crest of the hill. Believing that they had gained the rear

Confederate dead at the foot of the Round Tops.

of the Maine regiment, they found that the element of surprise had been reversed. In place of the enemy's backs, they encountered the exploding muzzles of Union rifles. Years later, Oates plainly summed up the effect of this fire on his command, "It was the most destructive I ever saw."

The Quiet Man

For the next hour or so, the Confederates, mostly men of the 15th and 47th Alabama regiments, held Chamberlain's regimental front in place while repeatedly attacking his left. They hoped to drive him away or gain his rear. As his men fell around him and the enemy closed in, Chamberlain walked calmly behind his line to reassure it of its work. One of the Alabamians later remembered that he fired directly at him, only to see another man save his life by stepping accidently in front. Two other enemy bullets, however, found their mark.

The first hit a rock at the base of one of Chamberlain's feet, tearing a gash in his right instep. The second hit the steel scabbard of his sword and badly bruised his left thigh. However, Chamberlain did not surrender. Despite the strain of his still-lingering fever, his inexperience, the worries of his command, his exposed flank and now two painful wounds, he held his place.

Colonel William C. Oates, 15th Alabama

Though the circumstances were oppressive, Chamberlain never showed his men a hint of hesitation or uncertainty. One of the most important lessons he learned from Ames and his own limited experience was the importance of the regiment's leader. A unit's strength was directly related to the coolness and confidence of its commander (or at least the outward demonstration of these crucial qualities).

"Up and down the line," one soldier recalled, "with a last word of encouragement or caution walks the quiet man, whose calm exterior concealed the fire of the warrior and the heart of steel, whose careful dispositions and ready resource, whose unswerving courage and audacious nerve in the last desperate crisis steadied the regiment…"

In an hour of intense fighting, the combatants fired more than thirty thousand bullets. One Alabamian remembered that "the blood stood in puddles on the rocks." Chamberlain himself remembered that, "The edge of conflict swayed to and fro, with wild whirlpools and eddies. At times I saw around me more of the enemy than of my own men: gaps opening, swallowing, closing again with sharp convulsive energy."

Bayonet!

At a critical juncture of the battle, he realized the enemy was close to victory. His own men were running out of ammunition and he could no longer hold the defensive position. However, his orders and the potential outcome of the entire battle forbade him from withdrawing. That is when, above the din of the battle, a thought formed in his crowded mind. He felt if his men could charge down the hill and disrupt the enemy in a surprise attack, then they might succeed in driving them back, perhaps away from the hill altogether. The thought barely had time to form. He called out, "Bayonet!" But by then, the action had commenced of its own accord. It began to the left, as the depleted line made a rush down the slope. With surging momentum, the charge grew until it swept down the hill. The onslaught drove away the Confederates. Dozens of others surrendered where they stood.

It was a glorious success. By the time the Maine men halted, they had propelled two regiments from the field and thrown back the Confederate attack hundreds of yards into the woods. Not that it occurred without some close moments. Running down the hill on his two injured legs, Chamberlain, with the regimental flag, faced an Alabama officer leveling a pistol at him. He fired from little more than six feet away. By some miracle, the bullet missed. Chamberlain took the officer as his prisoner by the point of his sword.

Almost immediately, soldiers and officers from nearby regiments recognized the maneuver and its importance. The brigade commander, now Colonel James Rice after the death of Strong Vincent, greeted him warmly, saying, "Colonel Chamberlain, your gallantry was magnificent, and your coolness and skill saved us." A lifetime of praise for a remarkable, improbable achievement followed.

A Night on Big Round Top

Chamberlain's work for the day was not finished. As the light escaped from the sky that evening, he was forced to consider a larger, heavily wooded hill. Years later, the hill would be named "Big Round Top," in deference to the smaller hill he held, which would be named "Little Round Top." Then, it was simply a huge forbidding place from which the enemy could threaten the tenuous Union line. Unable to convince a fresh brigade of Pennsylvania reserves to climb and capture the hill, Chamberlain's commander turned to him and asked if he would take it. Chamberlain immediately agreed.

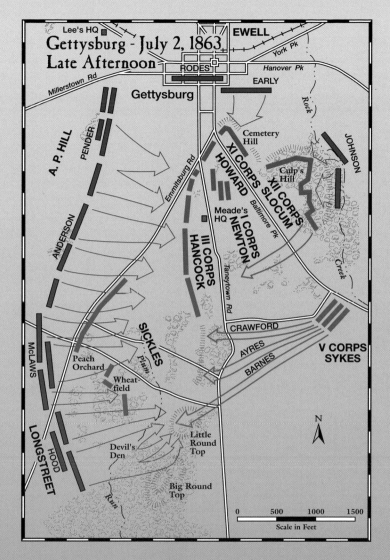

The 20th Maine Infantry was a member of Colonel Strong Vincent's 3rd Brigade of
Brigadier General James Barnes's First Division of Major General George Sykes's Fifth Army
Corps. After Major General Daniel Sickles's 3rd Army Corps abandoned its position on Little
Round Top and moved to the Peach Orchard area, the Fifth Corps came to its support.
Meanwhile, Confederate Lieutenant General James Longstreet's 1st Corps assaulted the
southern end of the Union line.

Joshua L. Chamberlain, wearing the brigadier general's star he was to earn at Petersburg.

NATIONAL ARCHIVES

ALTHOUGH MANY HISTORIANS speculate that Chamberlain planned and executed a "textbook military maneuver" at Gettysburg, his writings and those of his men suggest a somewhat different tale. At the high point of the crisis, when his line thinned and his men ran low on ammunition, Chamberlain probably thought of the idea to charge, but managed to inform only one of his officers.

An observer later described the maneuver as a "great right wheel swinging as if a gate on a post." But the men who initiated it, those on the left of the regiment, remembered no orders or directions. They recalled that the line began to move and they joined in the movement. At that end of line, the men focused on the enemy below and did not concern themselves with anything much more than five feet away. By all accounts the sounds of the battle were deafening. This, coupled with the fear and the adrenaline of combat, made an organized maneuver over rocks and through trees quite impossible.

As the men on the left described it—and the Alabamians across from them agreed—they started to move forward, slowly at first. However, confusion over movements in the line caused the surge, not an order to charge. When they reached the hillside, they spotted some of their Confederate attackers below and gave chase.

Just before the charge, the Alabama commander Colonel William Oates realized that he could not take the hill. His men were exhausted. They had marched more than two dozen miles that day, climbed Big Round

Top, fought for an hour with heavy casualties and ran low on ammunition. Oates's brother and best friend were mortally wounded as they fought beside him. Dusk was about to cover the battlefield. He needed to regroup.

Oates sent messengers to his men with the order to "run back the way they came" when he gave the signal. As the Maine men on the left wing came upon them, the Confederates assumed that Oates sent the signal. The chase commenced. While dozens of them dropped loaded rifles and surrendered, many escaped to the safety of the woods on Big Round Top. In the confusion of the attack, the Maine men grabbed as many prisoners as they could while pursuing the enemy "back the way they came." This, by the nature of the hill and the fight, meant that they moved in a direction that looked like a "gate swinging on a post." It was not a textbook military maneuver, just soldiers chasing their enemy in the direction that they ran.

At numerous events and in all of his writings, Chamberlain admitted that he never gave the actual order to charge. His men acted bravely on their own in the final moments of the battle. "It were vain to order 'forward,'" he later recalled. "No one would have heard it in the mighty Hosannah winging the sky."

Controversy surrounds the discussions of whether Chamberlain ever shouted the order "Charge!" Ironically, this debate clouds the real issue of his success at Gettysburg. The fact that Chamberlain, so stricken with illness, inexperience, concern for his men and his position, wounded in both legs, carried out his duties coolly, calmly and with great skill, is remarkable. Many great men have failed at much less.

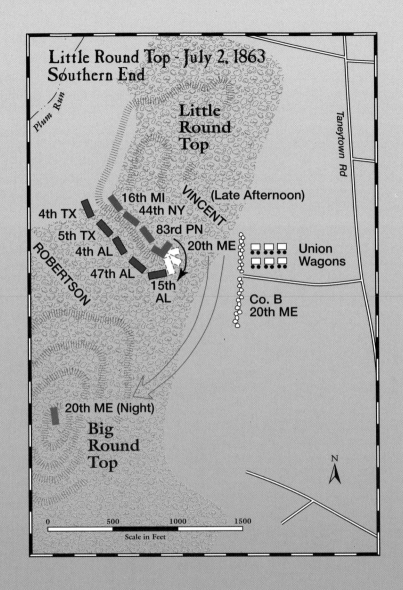

Little Round Top - July 2, 1863
Southern End

Plum Run

Little
Round
Top

VINCENT (Late Afternoon)

16th MI
44th NY
4th TX
5th TX   83rd PN
4th AL   20th ME   Union
                                 Wagons
ROBERTSON   47th AL
             15th
             AL   Co. B
                                 20th ME

Taneytown Rd

20th ME (Night)
Big
Round
Top

N

0   500   1000   1500
Scale in Feet

*After struggling for forty-five minutes with the 15th and 47th Alabama Infantry regiments
for Little Round Top, the 20th Maine ran low on ammunition. A bayonet charge, led by the
left, or southeast facing section of the line, swung to the northwest, like "a door on a hinge,"
sweeping the retreating Confederates before it.*

"I called for the colors," he remembered of his return to the regiment just then, "and asked for volunteers...every man sprang to his feet." Still, counting "every man," less than two hundred armed soldiers were prepared for the task. In heavy darkness, with little or no ammunition, they spread themselves thinly so they could uncover any of the enemy in the woods. The remnants of the regiment started the climb. After a few dozen fitful minutes, they reached a level area near the summit. They prostrated themselves on the ground. For all they knew, the entire Confederate army was just ahead in the darkness. Every noise seemed like the enemy approaching. Once, somebody yelled, "fire" and bullets flew in nearly every direction. One Mainer felt a missile fly near his cheek.

That night was charged with fear and danger. Years later, one officer in the regiment, remembering that evening, recalled to a friend that he was never as scared in all his life as he was that night on Big Round Top. As it turned out, the regiment had little to fear. A badly disabled Confederate army had neither the means nor the understanding of the situation. They could not mount a serious attack. Fearing the worst for his men, though, Chamberlain requested the help of two other regiments from his

USAMHI

The slopes of Big Round Top as seen from Devil's Den.

brigade. They soon came up to support him. By morning, he realized that they had escaped the danger with relative ease.

In the midst of that night's confusing hours, a group of men approached the Maine position. The nervous defenders ordered a halt. Responding to the usual, "who goes there," one of the approaching group replied, "Why, we're 4th Texas." To this a quick-witted Mainer returned, "All right, come on in.

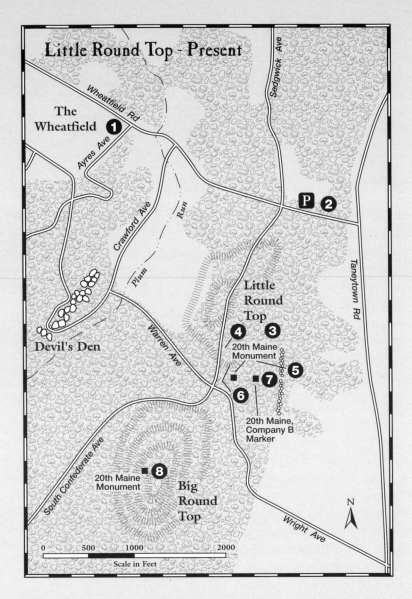

Little Round Top - Present

The Wheatfield ❶

Wheatfield Rd

Sedgwick Ave

Ayres Ave

Crawford Ave

Plum Run

🅿 ❷

Taneytown Rd

Little Round Top

❹ ❸
20th Maine Monument

■ ■ ❼ ❺

❻

20th Maine, Company B Marker

Warren Ave

Devil's Den

South Confederate Ave

20th Maine Monument ■ ❽

Big Round Top

N

Wright Ave

0 500 1000 2000
Scale in Feet

Chamberlain and the 20th Maine are forever linked with Little Round Top and the Battle of Gettysburg. The map, which corresponds with the tour featured in this section, follows the men from Maine as they fought each stage of the Battle of Gettysburg.

Aerial view of the Wheatfield, Gettysburg.

1 The 20th Maine arrived on the field at the eastern edge of the Wheatfield and immediately went to the hill later named Little Round Top.

2 Joshua, Tom and John Chamberlain rode up to the hill together. Behind them an enemy cannon shot exploded. Joshua, the eldest brother, sent John ahead to help set up a temporary field hospital and Tom to the rear of their marching column to assist the men. The 20th Maine then used an old logging trail to reach the summit from the protected reverse slope. That trail no longer exists.

3 John Chamberlain, a civilian traveling with his brothers and their regiment, helped set up a field hospital in a low protected place among the rocks well below the crest of the hill. Here, among a cluster of protective boulders, dozens of men received treatment for wounds. The regiment buried more than half a dozen of its own men.

4 The 20th Maine took its position as the last regiment in the Union line. Its battle line hugged the crest of the smaller offshoot of Little Round Top, later named "Vincent's Spur" in honor of the brigade commander who fell mortally wounded nearby. The remainder of the brigade fought in line across the modern road, facing more west than the 20th Maine's southerly and

Vincent's Spur, smaller offshoot of Little Round Top. Named for General Strong Vincent, who fell mortally wounded here.

easterly front. In 1886, officers of the regiment commissioned a monument to be built in Maine and shipped to Gettysburg. Today the monument stands at this site. Surrounding the 20th Maine's position is an old path. This is what remains of "Chamberlain Avenue" built in 1902. Use of the road by motor vehicles is discontinued.

❺ Near defeat, low on ammunition and outnumbered by the enemy, the 20th Maine charged down the hill into surprised Alabama troops. Stunned, these Confederates surrendered in droves. The charge began behind what is now the 20th Maine monument and swept around it to its front (toward the west).

❻ Just above the modern parking area an Alabama officer confronted Joshua Chamberlain. He fired at his face, just six feet away. Amazingly, the shot missed and Chamberlain took him prisoner.

❼ About 500 feet southeast of the 20th Maine memorial is another monument marking the position of its Company B. Just before the fight commenced, Chamberlain sent this company out to act as skirmishers. After being cut off by the enemy, it remained behind a stone wall until near the end of the fighting. It joined in the climactic charge and helped drive off the Alabamians.

❽ Near the summit of the larger hill, Big Round Top, is another monument placed by the survivors of the regiment. This marks the position held by about 200 men who captured the hill alone, in the dark and low on ammunition.

For more information about the battle or the site, contact the park.

Gettysburg National Military Park
95 Taneytown Road
Gettysburg, Pennsylvania 17325

Web Address: www.nps.gov/gett/

Looking south along Chamberlain Avenue, built in 1902 and which is now closed to vehicle traffic. The camera position is near the left end of the 20th Maine's "V-shaped" position. The colors were located at the present site of the regiment's monument. The Confederates would have attacked from left to right in this photograph.

Major General George E. Pickett

We're 4th Texas, too." By morning, the Mainers had captured more than three dozen men by repeating this ruse.

The following day, the Southern war effort began to unravel. What is termed as the "High Water Mark of the Confederacy" started with the grandest charge of the war. The infamous "Pickett's Charge" raged that day, and the 20th Maine, now near the center rear of the army, heard from a half mile away the tremendous bombardment and the musket fire that followed. As one veteran later wrote in his history of the war, "The self-sacrificing valor of the 20th Maine, under the gallant leadership of Joshua L. Chamberlain...saved to the Union arms the historic field of Gettysburg. Had they faltered for one instant...there would have been no grand charge of Pickett, and "Gettysburg" would have been the mausoleum of departed hopes of the national cause."

Despite its heroic work, the war was far from over for the 20th Maine and its commander. Although Chamberlain returned home to recuperate from his illness and from the stress brought on by the battle, he quickly returned to the army. Before the summer ended, he left the 20th Maine to command his own brigade. By June of the following year, he was a seasoned leader. He gained another appointment. This new brigade consisted of a new and five veteran Pennsylvania regiments. As the brigade's commander, he gained the respect of his men and his superior officers.

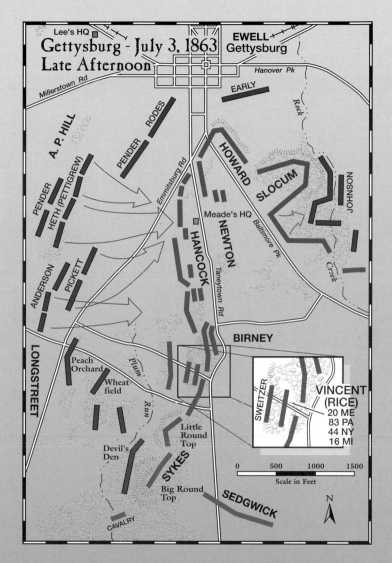

Gettysburg – July 3, 1863
Late Afternoon

Lee's HQ

EWELL
Gettysburg

Millerstown Rd

Hanover Pk

EARLY

A. P. HILL

PENDER   RODES

HOWARD

SLOCUM

JOHNSON

Rock

PENDER

HETH (PETTIGREW)

Emmitsburg Rd

Meade's HQ

HANCOCK

NEWTON

Baltimore Pk

Creek

ANDERSON

PICKETT

Taneytown Rd

BIRNEY

LONGSTREET

Peach
Orchard

Wheat
field

Plum

Run

SWEITZER

VINCENT
(RICE)
20 ME
83 PA
44 NY
16 MI

Devil's
Den

Little
Round
Top

SYKES

Big Round
Top

SEDGWICK

CAVALRY

0   500   1000   1500

Scale in Feet

N

After abandoning their position on Big Round Top, the 20th Maine and Vincent's Brigade
moved to a reserve position in the center of the Union line. After Vincent received a mortal
wound on July 2, Colonel James Rice of the 44th New York Infantry assumed command of
the brigade. While in the rear of Colonel Jacob Sweitzer's 2nd Brigade, Barnes's Division, it
did not partake in repulsing the assault known as Pickett's Charge.

SIEGE OF

7463

During the Siege of Petersburg, this huge piece of artillery earned the nickname, "The Dictator."

ON JUNE 18, 1864, Chamberlain and his new brigade arrived south of the Confederate capital of Richmond. They deployed on the battle lines near Petersburg. At a place known as Rives' Salient, Chamberlain surveyed the ominous line of

Petersburg

nemy entrenchments. The men and guns behind him gathered quickly. Chamberlain then

eceived a disturbing order, apparently from the staff of General Meade: his brigade was to

ttack the enemy position immediately.

CHAMBERLAIN WAS SHOCKED. He had watched the growing forces across from him strengthen their position. He could not believe that he received an order to attack across a wide open area in plain view of enemy guns. He pressed the messenger, saying, "Do they send a verbal order and say nothing about whether I am to make the attack alone, or with the whole army?" The messenger replied solemnly, "I understand you are to attack alone."

Still dumfounded by what seemed clearly to be a grievous error of command, Chamberlain quickly scribbled a note to Meade seeking more details. The tone of the missive was almost questioning. An officer returned shortly with mixed news. Chamberlain's audacity had not gotten him arrested, but he was, in fact, ordered to make the charge. He found some comfort in the news that the rest of the army would follow with him.

Chamberlain did not want to order his men to make the charge in front of him. He dismounted and handed the reins of his horse to an aide. After a brief patriotic speech, he stepped in front of the line, drew his sword and started toward the enemy works. They moved first at a march, then a jog and finally at a full run. Chamberlain led the way by a few steps.

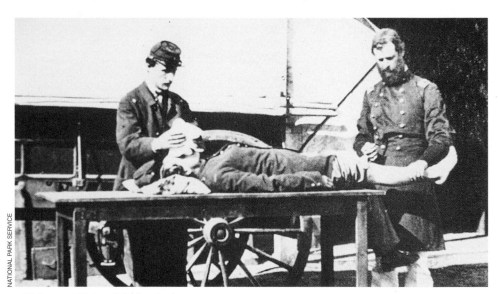

Unknown Union field hospital

74

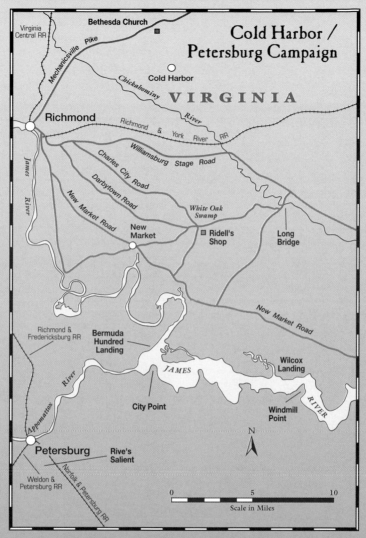

While the Confederates were handing Grant a defeat at Cold Harbor on June 3, 1864, Chamberlain was at Bethesda Church fighting his last battle with the 20th Maine. Later in the month, Grant attempted to capture Petersburg and its railroads. During the frantic battle on June 18, Chamberlain received a near mortal wounding at Rive's Salient. When the battle ended, both sides settled into a stalemate which lasted nine and one-half months. Chamberlain returned at the end of the siege, only to be wounded again on March 29, 1865. The siege ended a few days later when Lee, low on supplies and men, evacuated Petersburg and Richmond.

EARLY IN THE WAR, THE SOUTH realized that if Petersburg fell to the enemy, it would lose the war in the east. The major railroad lines which supplied Richmond and the troops in the field from points south, ran through Petersburg. After Major General George B. McClellan threatened Richmond in 1862, Confederate authorities commissioned field fortifications around Petersburg. The "Dimmock Line," as it became known, extended for ten miles around the town.

When Union troops captured City Point (now Hopewell, Virginia) in May 1864, the Confederates started shoring up the "Dimmock Line." After thirty days, Union forces arrived. Unsure of Confederate strength, they approached cautiously. Only a small group of Confederate reserves and second class militia manned the "Dimmock Line." More than half of them became casualties during the ensuing fight. But the remainder held on until Lee's army arrived.

Grant and his men reached Petersburg after being defeated soundly by Lee's men at Cold Harbor. Grant did not waver from his plan to capture Richmond, though. Petersburg was a key objective in that plan. Grant began assaults on the Confederate lines in earnest. The Siege of Petersburg began after a fierce battle on June 18, when both armies settled into a stalemate which lasted nine and one-half months.

Joshua L. Chamberlain at the Siege of Petersburg

On June 6 Chamberlain received word that he would finally have his own brigade. He left the 20th Maine to take charge of five small Pennsylvania regiments in a new First Brigade in Griffin's Division. They arrived in Virginia with the rest of the Army of the Potomac to take Petersburg.

The ferocious battle at Rive's Salient on June 18 proved difficult for Chamberlain. His flag bearer was killed, his horse was shot and he received confusing orders from his superiors. When the battle ended, about 2,000 men were counted as either died or wounded. Chamberlain was among them.

Chamberlain was severely wounded and thought to be dead. His brother Tom heard of his condition and sent for medical help. Some life-saving procedures were performed on him on the battlefield, and then he was taken to City Point. He survived the journey, and for the next three months convalesced at the Naval Academy

Union plans to blow gaps in the Confederate defenses around Petersburg ended with a tremendous explosion on July 30, 1864. A portion of "The Crater" can still be viewed east of the city.

Hospital in Annapolis. Because of his actions, General Grant appointed him to the rank of brigadier general. Chamberlain attempted numerous times to return to the battlefield, but his health stopped him. Eventually, he left for home to fully recover and did not return to the army until March 1865. He suffered from the wound until his death.

The End of the Siege
The Siege of Petersburg ended when the Confederate lines around Petersburg and Richmond stretched to the breaking point. Supplies ran low and manpower even lower. After a final Confederate assault on March 25, 1865, Lee realized the end was near. His attack on Fort Steadman lost almost 4,000 men, while Grant lost only 1,500. After April 1, at the Battle of Five Forks, Lee understood the futility of remaining in Petersburg. On April 2, he and his troops left their entrenchments. A week later, he surrendered his Army of Northern Virginia to Grant. The war was over in Virginia.

Points of Interest at Petersburg National Battlefield
Gowan Monument - Area where Chamberlain almost died on June 18, 1864.

Lewis Farm - Chamberlain received another serious wound here on March 29, 1865.

Information about the Park
Petersburg National Battlefield is on Highway 36 East. For more information about the siege and the site, contact the park.

Petersburg National Battlefield
1539 Hickory Hill Road
Petersburg, Virginia 23803

Web Address: www.nps.gov/pete/

Halfway to the Confederate line he realized that his men had to travel over rough terrain to reach their goal. He turned to give some commands. That is when his life took a significant and unfortunate turn.

Chamberlain Wounded

Chamberlain felt a sharp pain stab through his back. Feeling it, he fretted a moment over his honor, wondering, "What will my mother say, her boy shot in the back?" In a moment, however, the pain moved. A bullet had penetrated his right hip, tore through the center of his body, then rested against the other hip bone. He slumped slightly, using his sword to slow his fall. He managed to remain upright. He encouraged his men until they passed him. Once they moved on, he fell to one knee, then to the other, and finally, flat on the ground.

The next several hours remained a blur in Chamberlain's memory. Stretcher-bearers carried him through perilous musket and cannon fire. Less than twenty yards into the journey, a shell hit directly on the spot where he had just been. A large crater replaced the solid ground. His rescuers shook the dirt from the explosion and continued on. A musket ball then hit one of the carriers, breaking his arm. Finally, they reached a crude field hospital. Surgeons assessed the wound, declared it mortal and set

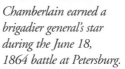

Chamberlain earned a brigadier general's star during the June 18, 1864 battle at Petersburg.

Captain Thomas Chamberlain

Chamberlain aside to die. Lying there with his life ebbing away, he bade farewell to fellow officers. He then instructed them to tell his men that they must continue to live up to their noble reputations. A number of ranking generals came to visit him. Two of them told him that they would recommend him for promotion to brigadier general.

Tom Chamberlain, now a captain with the 20th Maine, was nearby when he heard of his brother's wounding. He rushed to the hospital tent and upon discovering that the doctors had given up, went in search of aid. He returned without delay with two surgeons, including Dr. Abner Shaw of the 20th Maine. They learned that the bullet had severed blood vessels, broken bone and pierced his bladder. They tried to find the bullet by sliding the ramrod of a soldier's rifle through the wound, passing it through his body from one hip to the other. Recalling it later, he wrote, "I never dreamed what pain could be and not kill a man outright." They wanted to stop, believing that they were causing him unnecessary agony. Undaunted, he encouraged them to keep trying. They were able to piece enough of him together to warrant a slight hope for his survival.

From the aid station, a detail of six soldiers, ordered by the army's commander himself, set out on foot to carry him by stretcher. They took turns with the handles. After traveling sixteen miles under a hot sun, they placed him onto a ship that took him to a better-equipped hospital. Two days later he arrived at Annapolis, Maryland, where the government maintained a substantial facility for the care of wounded soldiers.

The New York papers printed his obituary. But he did not die. Though by his own description he arrived "'Booted and spurred', blood-soaked and smeared, hair and beard matted with blood and earth...pale as death and weak as water,"

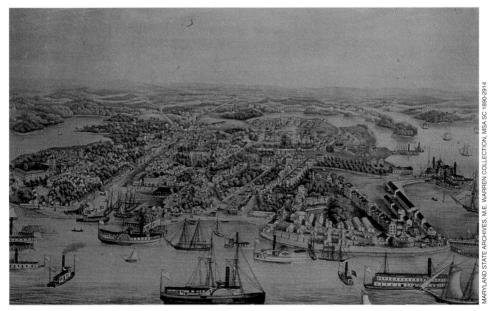

Sachse depiction of Annapolis, Maryland in 1865. St. John's College Hospital is viewed on the lower right side.

he slowly recovered. It is a grand testimony to his physical constitution that his "mortal" wound kept him out of the war but a few months.

Chamberlain could not even walk one hundred yards on his damaged hips. He experienced excruciating pain and should have stayed in Brunswick to recuperate. Instead, he returned to duty. While in the hospital, he received his promotion to brigadier general. He felt he could not let his men down. In November, he saddled up his horse Charlemagne, also recovering from an injury, and headed back to Petersburg.

Another Close Call

By now the outcome of the war was inevitable. However, the end was still months away, and there was much fighting and dying ahead. Despite the restrictions of his physical abilities, Chamberlain gallantly led his men in a number of charges. During one of them, he received another close call.

On March 29, 1865, on a byway called Quaker Road, Chamberlain was leading another assault on Confederate lines when he was shot again. This time, the bullet came through the neck of his horse, rattled up the sleeve of his coat, badly bruised his arm and struck him square in the breast. However, the bullet did not stop there. Chamberlain kept a

pack of papers and a small brass mirror in the breast pocket of his coat. The bullet struck a glancing blow off these articles and came out the side of his coat. It continued on until it struck and unseated an aide riding behind him. Chamberlain's comrades saw him slump unconscious against the horse's neck. He was covered in the animal's blood and they thought he was dead.

They were mistaken. After a short rest, Chamberlain recovered and before the

Lieutenant General Ulysses S. Grant

day ended, led his brigade in another charge. Riding madly around the field, he later recalled, "I hardly knew what world I was in." At one point in the confusion, he found himself surrounded by a small group of Confederate soldiers who leveled their rifles at him. He thought fast. He did not have his hat and wore an old faded coat, covered with mud and blood. He gave an idea a chance.

Looking sternly at the men who had demanded his surrender, he began to shout, "Surrender? What's the matter with you? What do you take me for? Don't you see those Yanks right on us?" Swiveling in the saddle, he then led the bewildered, but convinced soldiers in a charge back to his own line. There they were immediately taken prisoner.

Torrential rain forced a halt in the fighting for the better part of two days. When the weather cleared enough for men and horses to move, the conflict resumed. At first, the action did not go well for the Fifth Corps. Other brigades had been badly routed on the field. The enemy controlled an important road that Chamberlain and his brigade had captured days before. Chamberlain, still exhausted, took time to rest his failing body on a pile of sawdust near an old sawmill. However, at midday, General Warren rode up to the weakened

Major General Gouverneur K. Warren

commander and hastily explained the seriousness of the situation.

"General Chamberlain," he asked. "Will you save the honor of the Fifth Corps?" He needed a successful charge and had seen for himself what Chamberlain and his men could accomplish. While Chamberlain pondered his still painful wounds, Warren reinforced his request. "We have come to you," he said plainly. "You know what that means."

Moments later, Chamberlain climbed atop his wounded horse. Both were still filthy and spattered with each other's blood. They led the charge. With Robert E. Lee personally commanding the Confederates, Chamberlain and his men re-captured the road, drove 300 yards and captured an entire Virginia regiment. Even a Confederate officer recalled, "I thought it was one of the most gallant things I had ever seen."

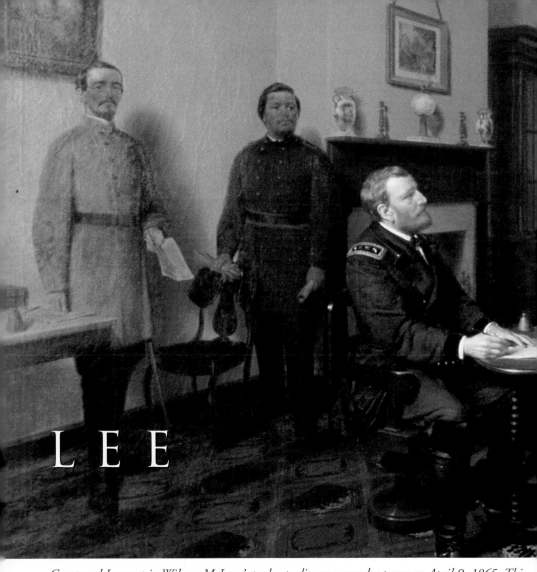

LEE

Grant and Lee met in Wilmer McLean's parlor to discuss surrender terms on April 9, 1865. This
describe Grant and Lee at separate tables across the room from each other.

BY THE SECOND WEEK OF APRIL, the Confederate army reached the end of it

strength. On April 9, 1865, at a small community called Appomattox Court House

Robert E. Lee surrendered the remnants of his once great army to Lieutenant General

surrenders

painting by L. M. D. Guilliame is considered inaccurate. Eyewitness accounts

Ulysses S. Grant. Three days later, the formal surrender ceremony took place. A long, dusty column of men in gray marched a few hundred yards to offer up their arms and their flags. As they did so, a Union line met them.

LIBRARY OF CONGRESS, COPY PRINT COURTESY OF THE MUSEUM OF THE CONFEDERACY, RICHMOND, VIRGINIA

Union plans to end the war centered around the Confederate capital, Richmond, Virginia. Near the end of the war, Lee evacuated the city and Union troops occupied it.

GRANT COULD HAVE CHOSEN an officer of higher rank to command the line. However, he hand-picked Joshua Chamberlain to accept the formal surrender of Lee's army. Grant never offered a thorough explanation for his choice. However, Chamberlain's heroic actions during the previous weeks must have weighed heavily in his favor.

When the formal ceremony began, Chamberlain sat upright on his horse. He watched regiment after regiment pass by. He ordered his men to a secondary form of salute for their vanquished foe. He knew that many in the North would be furious, but he did it nonetheless. Many years later he explained, "Before us in proud humiliation stood the embodiment of manhood...thin, worn, and famished, but erect, and with eyes looking level into ours, waking

memories that bound us together as no other bond;—was not such manhood to be welcomed back into a Union so tested and assured?"

Though Chamberlain never wavered from his belief in the appropriateness of his decision, it caused him some trouble. The act incensed the many Northerners who had lost relatives at the hands of these men. At the same time, others saw him as something of a hero. Many in the South considered him an "acceptable" Yankee. Historians have described the gesture as important in the healing process between the two sides.

Regardless of the surrender's effect, Chamberlain's military career essentially ended that day. Later he received a brevet major general's rank and months of recuperative medical care. But, it was time to return to a civilian's life. He traveled back to Brunswick.

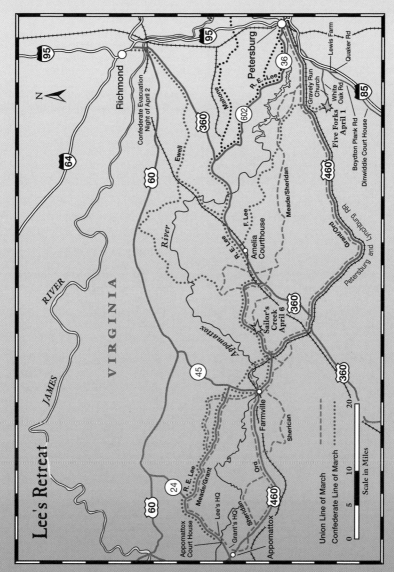

Lee's Retreat

Richmond

95

95

64

60

VIRGINIA

JAMES RIVER

RIVER

Petersburg

36

R. E. Lee

Mattoax

602

360

Confederate Evacuation
Night of April 2

Ewell

R. E. Lee

F. Lee

**Amelia
Courthouse**

Appomattox River

45

**Sailor's
Creek
April 6**

360

360

Farmville

Sheridan

Meade/Sheridan

460

R. E. Lee

Meade/Grant

Ora

Sheridan

24

60

**Appomattox
Court House**

Appomattox

Lee's HQ

Grant's HQ

460

85

Lewis Farm

Quaker Rd

White
Oak Rd

**Five Forks
April 1**

Boydton Plank Rd

Dinwiddie Court House

**Gravelly Run
Church**

**Richmond and
Lynchburg RR**

Petersburg and
Lynchburg RR

Union Line of March

Confederate Line of March

Scale in Miles

0   5   10   20

N

General Robert E. Lee and the Army of Northern Virginia left the trenches of Petersburg and Richmond to escape Grant and his superior numbers. For just over one week, they attempted to join another Confederate army in North Carolina, only to surrender at Appomattox Court House, Virginia on April 9, 1865. Joshua L. Chamberlain received the honor of officiating at the formal surrender ceremony on April 12.

NATIONAL PARK SERVICES

Wilmer McLean's house in Appomattox Court House.

THROUGHOUT JANUARY AND February, 1865, Lee's men remained caught in the trenches around Petersburg. Lee knew he had to evacuate, but muddy roads, unhealthy horses and a number of other unfavorable circumstances conspired to keep him grounded. The Confederates stayed in the trenches through March.

Grant took full advantage of Lee's predicament. On March 29, he moved Major General Philip Sheridan's cavalry and General Warren's Fifth Corps to the southwest. His forces crushed Pickett's at Five Forks. By April 2, he was prepared to set into motion an all-out offensive against the Confederates. Lee knew it was useless to stay any longer. He ordered Richmond and Petersburg evacuated on the night of April 2-3. He then headed for Amelia

Court House to regroup and obtain much-needed supplies.

Grant continued to put immense pressure on Lee's troops. Wherever they turned, he turned. The Confederate forces began to unravel. The men, weak from a lack of sleep and food, collapsed. The columns started to disintegrate. Lee continued to move, but his concern ever-increased. The final blow came on April 7. At Sailor's Creek, Union forces destroyed much of the Army of Northern Virginia's rear guard. Eight thousand men were either killed, wounded or captured. Lee moved on, but with only a slim hope of escape. Little could be done to stop the Union advance.

On April 7, Grant sent Lee a letter requesting surrender. Lee met with his trusted subordinates, but they refused to submit. They believed they could escape to North Carolina and General Joseph Johnston's army. Grant tried to help them understand the futility of that belief by fiercely pounding them at every turn. On April 9, near Appomattox Court House, Lee sent word to Grant that he would like to meet in order to discuss surrender terms. They met at the home of Wilmur McLean, and after four years, an agreement to end the hostilities was reached.

Surrender at Appomattox *by Ken Riley.*

Joshua L. Chamberlain at the Surrender

Grant chose Chamberlain to supervise the official surrender ceremony based on his efforts at Petersburg. Chamberlain decided ahead of time to acknowledge the defeated troops with a formal military salute. As he said in his biography, *The Passing of the Armies*, "The momentous meaning of this occasion impressed me deeply. I resolved to mark it by some token of recognition, which could be no other than a salute of arms. Before us in proud humiliation stood the embodiment of manhood: men whom neither toils and sufferings, nor the fact of death, nor disaster, nor hopelessness could bend from their resolve; standing before us now, thin, worn, and famished, but erect, and with eyes looking level into ours, waking memories that bound us together as no other bond;—was not such manhood to be welcomed back into a Union so tested and assured?"

The ceremony lasted all day on April 12, 1865.

Points of Interest at Appomattox Court House NHP

Richmond-Lynchburg Stage Road - Chamberlain lined his men along this road in order to accept the official surrender. The Confederates stacked their arms along the stretch of the road between the Peers House and the McLean House.

McLean House - The setting for the April 9 meeting between Grant and Lee. Formal surrender terms were approved and accepted here.

Information About the Park

Appomattox Court House National Historical Park is on Virginia State Highway 24, three miles northeast of the town of Appomattox, Virginia. For more information about the surrender and the site, contact the park.

Appomattox Court House NHP
PO Box 218
Appomattox, Virginia 24522

Web Address: www.nps.gov/apco/

AFTER

Capitol building in Augusta, Maine, 1880. Here, as commander of the state militia, Chamberlain

NEWS OF CHAMBERLAIN'S EXPLOITS from Gettysburg to Appomattox had not gone unnoticed by his fellow Mainers. Several months after the close of the war, they elected him governor for the first of four consecutive one-year terms. During his

the war

...pt order during an angrily disputed state election.

MAINE HISTORIC PRESERVATION COMMISSION

...enure, he sought to expand Maine's industrial and intellectual strength. The school he

...stablished for this purpose became the University of Maine.

89

Governor Chamberlain's office

W HEN HIS TERMS AS
governor ended, Chamberlain
accepted the presidency of Bowdoin
College. During the twelve years he
served at that post, he tried to
modernize the school's classical
curriculum. Occasionally he succeeded.
He added science and engineering
programs. He advocated the admission
of women to the school. Before he
retired, he personally taught every course
except mathematics.

While serving as Bowdoin's president,
Chamberlain realized that he needed a
home large enough to entertain guests
and visiting dignitaries. He did not want
to buy a larger house. He was
comfortable with his current one. So, he

Chamberlain at Bowdoin College's 1904 commencement. He is third from left.

Joshua L. Chamberlain's house in Brunswick, Maine after he added a new bottom floor.

decided to raise his modest Cape Cod style home some twenty feet in the air and build a large first floor beneath it. There he entertained President U. S. Grant and other prominent individuals. He even had the pleasure of showing it to the house's former occupant, Henry Wadsworth Longfellow.

Chamberlain occupied his later years overseeing relatively unsuccessful investments in Florida and New York. However, he became an extremely popular speaker and wrote many magazine and newspaper articles. He spoke frequently and shared the platform with many of the literary giants

Front and back view of Chamberlain's Medal of Honor

IN 1893, CHAMBERLAIN RECEIVED a package sent by parcel post from Washington, D.C. Inside was a letter from the United States Congress. With it was a Congressional Medal of Honor. Although it had been recommended based on his entire military career, the citation declared that the award was for his work at Gettysburg. It specifically cited his "daring heroism and great tenacity in holding his position on the Little Round Top against repeated assaults, and carrying the advance position on the Great Round Top."

Further acclaim followed. In 1902, President Theodore Roosevelt spoke in Portland, Maine. He mentioned Chamberlain's accomplishments. "...you, General, to whom it was given at the supreme moment of the war to win the supreme reward of a soldier...and may we keep ourselves from envying him because to him fell the supreme good fortune of winning the medal of honor for mighty deeds done in the mightiest battle that the nineteenth century saw."

Chamberlain's Medal of Honor is now a part of the Special Collections of Bowdoin College.

Chamberlain at the helm of his yacht with Lena Pool.

of his era. Eventually, he settled into a political retirement job as Surveyor at the Port of Portland, Maine. Fanny passed away in 1905 at the age of eighty.

Chamberlain served as one of the commissioners planning a grand reunion of soldiers at Gettysburg. He did so with great enthusiasm, despite his age and

20th Maine veterans return to Little Round Top to plan a monument. Chamberlain is standing third from left.

Chamberlain's headstone

failing health. The Petersburg wound constantly troubled him, making even simple tasks painful. He traveled to Gettysburg in May, 1913 for a planning meeting. It proved to be his last visit.

When Chamberlain returned home, his condition slowly worsened. Confined to his bed, his lungs failed and his old wound became infected. The physician who fifty years earlier had treated his wounds and saved his life, attended him. The end came quietly. During the cold morning of February 24, 1914, he died in his Portland home. Three days later, a huge funeral procession traveled through Portland and onto Brunswick. There, the "Hero of Little Round Top," four-term governor of Maine and president of Bowdoin College, was laid to rest. He designed the headstone himself. As he wished, it made no mention of his numerous accomplishments. It stated simply, "Joshua L. Chamberlain 1828 - 1914."

MANY ARGUE THAT MUCH OF Joshua Chamberlain's fame is based on his poignant and prolific writings. However, his fame and popularity preceded the widespread publication of his greatest, most often quoted works. Many veterans and prominent historical figures of his lifetime admired and respected him. He was often invited to give speeches and attend functions. Publishers did not print his writings until the years just before and after his death.

Two of the most often read accounts of Chamberlain's experiences in battle are full of errors and inventions and were not even fully written by him. *Hearst* and *Cosmopolitan* magazines published his "Through Blood and Fire at Gettysburg" and "My Story of Fredericksburg." William Randolph Hearst owned and controlled both magazines. He promoted "yellow journalism," which had a reputation for embellishing and creating outright fabrications in order to make stories more enjoyable for paying readers.

After he read the final forms, Chamberlain was angered. He refused to obtain copies for himself or for friends. When asked, he lamented that the Hearst people "mutilated my Gettysburg." He complained that they had added "connective tissue" to his words. A few of his old comrades, unaware of Hearst's tampering, believed that Chamberlain wrote the articles. They felt great dismay at some of the things they read, which exalted Chamberlain and his actions at the expense of his men.

It is ironic that some of the works most quoted by Chamberlain, and perhaps most responsible for his current popularity, may not be his after all. At the same time, the speeches and writings that made him popular with the people of his own time, are those least often cited by modern writers.

FURTHER READINGS

Suggestions for further reading about Joshua Lawrence Chamberlain

In the Hands of Providence: Joshua L. Chamberlain and the American Civil War. Alice Raines Trulock. University of North Carolina Press, 1992. The best biography of Chamberlain. Well-researched account details his war years and presents a brief history of his life after the war.

The 20th Maine: a Volunteer Regiment in the Civil War. John J. Pullen. J. B. Lippincott, 1957. Reprinted by Morningside Bookshop, 1997. Considered one of the best Civil War regimental histories ever written.

Stand Firm Ye Boys From Maine: the 20th Maine and the Gettysburg Campaign. Thomas A. Desjardin. Thomas Publications, 1995. Describes the regiment's movements through the entire Gettysburg Campaign. Uses more than seventy accounts to describe the fighting at Little Round Top.

Fanny and Joshua: the Enigmatic Lives of Fanny and Joshua Chamberlain. Diane Monroe Smith. Thomas Publications, 1999. Fascinating analysis of the Chamberlains' very complicated relationship. Chamberlain scholars agree that his relationship with Fanny profoundly affected his entire life.

Joshua Chamberlain: a Hero's Life and Legacy. John J. Pullen. Stackpole, 1999. Wonderful description and analysis of the last two decades of Chamberlain's life, including his years as governor of Maine and president of Bowdoin College.

The Chamberlains of Brewer. Diana H. Loski. Thomas Publications, 1999. Concise study of the Chamberlain siblings.

Through Blood and Fire at Gettysburg. Joshua L. Chamberlain. Reprinted by Stan Clark Military Books, 1994. The 1913 account written for and by *Hearst* magazine with added illustrations.

The Passing of the Armies. Joshua L. Chamberlain. Reprinted by Stan Clark Military Books, 1994. The 1915 account of the Petersburg and Appomattox Campaigns.